Photograph of Richard Wagner, signed and inscribed
to Mrs. Gustav Schirmer, wife of the
founder of the house.

THE MASTERSINGERS
OF NUREMBERG

An Opera in Three Acts

Music by
RICHARD WAGNER

**Complete Vocal Score in a
Facilitated Arrangement by**
KARL KLINDWORTH

English Translation by
FREDERICK JAMESON

Ed. 1697

G. SCHIRMER, Inc.

DISTRIBUTED BY

HAL•LEONARD
CORPORATION
7777 W. BLUEMOUND RD. P.O. BOX 13819 MILWAUKEE, WI 53213

CHARACTERS

HANS SACHS, Shoemaker	. . . . .	*Bass*
VEIT POGNER, Goldsmith	. . . . .	*Bass*
KUNZ VOGELGESANG, Furrier	. . . . .	*Tenor*
KONRAD NACHTIGALL, Tinsmith	. . . . .	*Bass*
SIXTUS BECKMESSER, Town Clerk	. . . . .	*Bass*
FRITZ KOTHNER, Baker	. .	*Bass*
BALTHASAR ZORN, Pewtere.	. .	*Tenor*
ULRICH EISSLINGER, Grocer	. . . . .	*Tenor*
AUGUSTIN MOSER, Tailor	. . . . .	*Tenor*
HERMANN ORTEL, Soap-maker	. . . . .	*Bass*
HANS SCHWARZ, Stocking-weaver	. . . . .	*Bass*
HANS FOLTZ, Coppersmith	. . . . .	*Bass*

Mastersingers

WALTHER VON STOLZING, a Young Knight from Franconia *Tenor*

DAVID, Sachs's 'Prentice . . . . *Tenor*

EVA, Pogner's Daughter . . . . *Soprano*

MAGDALENA, Eva's Attendant . . . . *Soprano*

A NIGHT-WATCHMAN . . . . *Bass*

Men and Women of all Guilds, Journeymen, 'Prentices, Girls, Folk

SCENES OF THE ACTION

FIRST ACT: *The Interior of St. Katharine's Church*

SECOND ACT: *In the streets, before the houses of Pogner and Sachs*

THIRD ACT: (Scs. I-IV) *Sachs's workshop*, (Sc. V) *An open meadow on the Pegnitz*

PLACE: *Nuremberg*

TIME: *About the middle of the sixteenth century*

LIST OF SCENES

In the English version of the text, all names of persons (even those of Walther, David, and Eva), and all exclamations, except where they are obviously English, should be pronounced as in German.

Die Meistersinger von Nürnberg

von
RICHARD WAGNER.

Vorspiel.

Klavierauszug
von Karl Klindworth.

27327 c

2

27327

4

Bewegt, doch immer noch etwas breit.

molto cresc.

più f

ff

molto espressivo la melodia

p

mf e marcato

10

27827

Sehr feurig.

Erster Aufzug.
Erste Scene.

Die Bühne stellt das Innere der Katharinenkirche in schrägem Durchschnitt dar; von dem Hauptschiff, welches links ab, dem Hintergrunde zu, sich ausdehnend anzunehmen ist, sind nur noch die letzten Reihen der Kirchenstühlbänke sichtbar: den Vordergrund nimmt der freie Raum vor dem Chor ein; dieser wird später durch einen schwarzen Vorhang gegen das Schiff zu gänzlich geschlossen.
In der letzten Reihe der Kirchenstühle sitzen Eva und Magdalena; Walther von Stolzing steht, in einiger Entfernung, zur Seite an eine Säule gelehnt, die Blicke auf Eva heftend, die sich mit stummen Gebärdenspiel wiederholt zu ihm umkehrt.

First Act.
First scene.

The stage represents an oblique view of the church of St. Katharine; the last few rows of seats of the nave, which is on the left stretching towards the back, are visible: in front is the open space of the choir which is later shut off from the nave by a black curtain.
In the last row of seats Eva and Magdalena sit; Walther von Stolzing stands at some distance at the side leaning against a column with his eyes fixed on Eva, who frequently turns round towards him with mute gestures.

27327

tod,
lease,

gab er uns des Heil's Ge-
teach-ing us his law of

tod,
lease,

gab er uns des Heil's Ge-
teach-ing us his law of

tod,
lease,

gab er uns des Heil's ___ Ge-
teach-ing us his law of

tod,
lease,

gab er uns des Heil's Ge-
teach-ing us his law of

(Walther zärtlich, dann dringender.)
(Walther, tenderly, then more urgently.)
sehr ausdrucks. *molto cresc.* *f dlm.*
p

bot,
peace,

dass wir durch sein'
let us share thy

bot,
peace,

dass wir durch sein'
let us share thy

bot,
peace,

dass wir durch sein'
let us share thy

bot,
peace,

dass wir durch sein'
let us share thy

(Eva, Walthern schüchtern abweisend, aber schnell wieder seelenvoll zu ihm aufblickend.)
(Eva shyly repels Walther, but quickly looks up at him again with emotion.)
cresc. *f dim.*
p *cresc.* *p*

20

(Da Walther Eva sich nähern sieht, drängt er sich gewaltsam durch die Kirchgänger zu ihr.)
(*Walther, seeing Eva coming, presses forcibly through the crowd to her.*)

EVA (sich schnell zu Magdalene umwendend.)
(*turning round quickly to Magdalena.*)

Mein Brauttuch, schau!
My kerchief, look!

WALTHER.

Verweilt!   Ein Wort!   ein einzig Wort!
Oh stay!   *A word!*   *one single word!*

Lebhafter.

EVA.

Wohl liegt's im Ort _   MAGDALENA (Sie geht nach den Kirchstühlen zurück.)
'Tis left be-hind _   (*She goes back to the seats.*)

Vergesslich Kind!   Nun heisst es: such'!
Forget-ful child!   *Now I must seek!*

WALT.

Licht und Lust, o-der Nacht und Tod? Ob ich er-fahr, wo-nach ich ver-
light and life, or night and death_ whether I learn the tid-ings I

lan - ge, ob ich ver-neh- - me, wo-vor mir graut:_ mein Fräu-lein,
hope for, whether I hear what sore-ly I dread:_ fair maid-en

MAGD. (Wieder zurückkommend.)
(Returning again.)

Da ist auch die Spange._ Komm, Kind! Nun hast du Spang' und Tuch....
There hast thou the buckle._ Come child! Now hast thou clasp and scarf.

sagt....
say...

(Sie geht nochmals eilig nach hinten.)
(She goes again hastily to the back.)

O weh! da ver-gass ich selbst mein Buch!
A - lack! now I have for-got my book!

MAGD.

Hel-den   ich Meister Pogner mel-den? **WALT** (bitter leidenschaftlich) Ei! Jun-ker, was
com-ing   as guest to Master Pog-ner? (with passionate bitterness.) Sir knight, ah what

O, be-trat ich doch nie sein Haus!
Would that ne'er I had seen his house!

sagt ihr da aus?   In Nürnberg eben nur an gekom-men, war't ihr nicht freundlich
words do I hear?   In Nüremberg, tho' so new a com-er, have you not found all

auf-genommen?   Was Küch' und Keller, Schrein und Schrank euch bot, ver-dient' es keinen
friendly welcome?   What kitchen, cellar, hearth and house could give, doth that deserve no

EVA.

Gut Len'chen, ach! das mein er ja nicht; doch von mir wohl wünscht er Be-richt,_ wie sag' ich's
Good Lene, ah, he means it not so; but from me now fain would he know,_ 'tis hard to

Dank?
thanks?

28

MAGD.

wohl noch Nie-mand kennt, bis morgen ihn das Ge-richt er-nennt, das dem Mei - - ster-
truth the bridegroom's name, un-til to - morrow shall sound his fame, when a mas - -ter-

marcato

staccato

EVA (enthusiastisch)
(enthusiastically)

Und selbst__ die Braut ihm reicht das Reis.
And him ___ the bride her - self will crown.

sin - ger er-theilt den Preis…
sin-ger the prize hath won…

cresc.

p staccato

EVA.

(bang.)
(anxiously)

Seid ihr das nicht?
Are you not that?

WALT. (verwundert)
(surprised)

Dem Mei - ster-sin-ger?
A mas - ter-sin-ger?

27327

Zweite Scene.

Second Scene.

klin-gend, was Maas, was Zahl,— den Lei-sten im Schurz, was lang, was
learn a-bout time and beat— with lap-stone and last, the slow, the

kurz, was hart, was lind, hell o-der blind, was Wai-sen was Myl-ben, was Kleb-
fast, the hard, the light, gloom-y and bright, the scissors and snippings, and word-

syl-ben, was Pau-sen, was Kör-ner, was Blu-men, was Dör-ner,— das
clippings, the pau-ses and corns, the flowers and thorns, I

al-les lernt' ich mit Sorg' und Acht: wie weit nun, meint ihr, dass ich's ge-
learn all such things with care and pains: to what now think you all this at-

50

WALTH.

Wohl zu'nem Paar recht gu-ter Schuh?
Say, to a pair of right good shoon?

DAV.

bracht?
tains?

DAV.

Ja, da - hin hat's noch gu - te Ruh! Ein „Bar" hat manch' Gesätz' und Ge-
Ah, think not that is reached so soon! A "Bar" of ma - ny stan-zas is

bänd': wer da gleich die rech-te Re - gel fänd', die richt' - ge Nath und den
made: and the rules a-lone would break your head, and right - ly stitched and

rech - ten Drath, mit gut ge-füg - ten Stol - len den Bar recht zu—ver-
tru - ly pitched must words and mu - sic an - swer, when bar is soled with

27327

DAV.

soh - len! Und dann erst kommt der Ab-gesang, dass der nicht kurz und nicht zu lang, und auch
stan - za! Then com - eth first the After-song, and not too short nor yet too long; and in

kei - nen Reim ___ ent - hält, ___ der schon im Stollen ge -
it ___ no rhyme ___ may sound ___ that in the stan-za is

stellt. Wer al - les das merkt, weiss und kennt, wird doch immer noch nicht
found. Who all this has read, marked and learned hath e'en yet the name of

WALTH. **Schneller.**

Hilf Gott! Will ich denn Schu-ster sein?
Odd's life! Teach me not cobbler's trade?

Mei - ster ge - nennt.
Mas - ter not earned. **Schneller.**

WALTH.

In die Singkunst lie-ber führ'mich ein!
Rather tell me how a singer's made!

DAV.

Ja— hätt' ich's nur selbst schon zum Singer ge-
Ah, would that a sing-er al-ready I

dolce

p

p

bracht! Wer glaubt wohl, was das für Mü - he macht!
were! Who know-eth what time that needs and care!

cresc. - - sf

tranq. dolce

f dim. *p*

Der Mei - ster Tön' und Wei - sen, gar viel an
The Mas - ters' tones and mea - sures are ma-ny in.

p

Nam' und Zahl, die star - ken, und die lei - sen, wer die wüss - te
name and kind; the strong ones and the soft ___ ones, who at once their

f *p*

dolce

P. + P. +

27827

klingen, wo steigt die Stimm', und wo sie fällt; fangt nicht zu hoch, zu tief nicht an, als es die
ringing, as voice doth rise and fall at need; start not too high, too low in pitch, but where the

cresc.
f
p

Stimm' er - rei - chen kann. Mit dem A - them spart, dass er nicht
voice all notes can reach. To the breath give heed and hold it

p

knappt und gar am End' ihr ü - berschnappt; vor dem Wort mit der Stim - me ja nicht
well, lest at the end your voice should fail. Ere a word you pronounce, make not a

cresc.
f
p

summt, nach dem Wort mit dem Mund auch nicht brummt. Nicht än - dert an
groan, when the word ends, the voice may not moan; and al - ter not

più p

58 DAV.

27327

60

27327

DAVID.

füg-tet ihr selbst nun Reim' und Wort, dass sie ge-nau an Stell' und Ort pass-ten
if you yourself both rhyme and word find and unite in true ac-cord, so that

p

dolce

zu ei - nes Mei-sters Ton:_ dann _____ trägt ihr den Dich - - ter-preis da -
they fit some Master's tone: then _____ you've made the Po - - et's prize your

cresc.

f

von.
own.

ALT.

1ᵗ TENOR.

LEHRBUBEN.
PRENTICES.

He! Da-vid! soll man's dem Mei - ster kla-gen? Wirst' dich
Hey! Da-vid! must we then tell thy master? Wilt thou

2ᵗ TENOR.

Soll man's kla - gen?
Shall we tell him

ff (lärmend)

f f f

P.

27327

66

(Die Lehrbuben, welche in der Mitte der Bühne ein grosses Gerüste mit Vorhängen aufgeschlagen hatten, schaffen auf Davids Weisung dies schnell bei Seite, und stellen dafür ebenso eilig ein geringeres Bretter- gerüst auf; darauf stellen sie einen Stuhl, mit einem kleinen Pult davor, daneben eine grosse schwarze Tafel, daran die Kreide am Faden aufgehängt wird; um das Gerüst sind schwarze Vorhänge angebracht welche zunächst hinten und an den beiden Seiten, dann auch vorn ganz zusammengezogen werden.)

(The Prentices, who had put up a large erection with curtains in the middle of the stage, put it aside under David's directions and substitute for it a smaller stage; on this they place a chair with a small desk before it, near it a large black board on which a piece of chalk is hung by a string; around the stage are hung black curtains which are pulled together first at the back and sides and then in front.)

27827

LEHRBUBEN.
PRENTICES.

singt er glatt!
knows by heart!

singt er glatt!
knows by heart!
Doch die har-te Tritt-weis',
And the hearty - kick-mode
die
he

singt er glatt!
knows by heart!

f stacc.   p   stacc.   f   p

(mit der Gebärde zweier Fusstritte.)
(with the action of two kicks.)

die   trat ihm der Meis-ter   hart und   fest.
his   mas-ter em-ploys them   all   by   turns. (Sie lachen.)
(They laugh.)

kennt er am best'; die   trat ihm der Meis-ter   hart und   fest.
care-ful-ly learns, his   mas-ter em-ploys them   all   by   turns.

die   trat ihm der Meis-ter   hart und   fest.
his   mas-ter em-ploys them   all   by   turns.

cresc. - - -   f   ff

DAV.

Ja, lacht nur zu! Heut' bin ich's nicht.
Yes, laugh a - way! *but not at me.*

Ein And'- rer stellt sich zum Ge-richt; der war nicht Schüler, ist nicht
There comes an - o - ther,_ you will see; no scholar is he, singer

Singer, den Dichter, sagt er, ü - ber-spring'er; denn er ist Jun-ker, und mit einem
neither; the po-et's place he wants not ei-ther: a noble knight, he,_in a single

Sprung er denkt, oh - ne weit're Beschwerden heut' hier Meister zu wer - den. D'rum
flight he hopes without let or dis-as-ter here to-day to be Mas - ter. Then

27327

DAV.

(während die Lehrbuben vollends aufrichten.)
(while the prentices finish the erection.)

rich - tet nur fein das Ge-merk dem ein! Dort-hin!
work ye right well at the mark-er's cell! Thith-er!

Hier-her!
Hith-er!

Die Ta - fel an die Wand,_
The tab-let on the wall,_

(zu Walther sich umwendend.)
(turning to Walther.)

so dass sie recht dem Merker zur Hand!_ Ja, ja, dem
that so the Mark-er's hand on it fall!_ Aye, aye, the

dim. p

Mer - ker!_ Wird euch wohl bang? Vor ihm_ schon_
*Mark - er!_ Do you grow pale? Be - fore_ him_*

Etwas zurückhaltend.

pp

72

27327

LEHR.BUBEN.
PRENTICES.

Blu-menkränzlein aus Sei-den fein, wird das dem Herrn Ritter be - schie - - - den
silk- en chaplet of flowers bright will that by good fortune be yours,_____ sir

Blu-menkränzlein aus Sei-den fein, wird das dem Herrn Ritter be-schie - - - den
silk- en chaplet of flowers bright will that by good fortune be yours,_____ sir

Blu-menkränzlein aus Sei-den fein, wird das dem Herrn Ritter be - schie - - - den
silk- en chaplet of flowers bright will that by good fortune be yours,_____ sir

sein?
knight?
(Die Lehrbuben fahren sogleich erschrocken auseinander, als die Sacristei aufgeht und Pogner
(The Prentices separate in alarm as the sacristy opens and Pogner with Beckmesser enters;

sein?
knight?

sein?
knight?

mit Beckmesser eintritt; sie ziehen sich nach hinten zurück.)
they retire to the back.)

Dritte Scene.

(Die Einrichtung ist nun folgender Massen beendigt:— zur Seite rechts sind gepolsterte Bänke in der Weise aufgestellt, dass sie einen schwachen Halbkreis nach der Mitte zu bilden. Am Ende der Bänke, in der Mitte der Bühne, befindet sich das „Gemerk" benannte Gerüste, welches zuvor hergerichtet worden. Zur linken Seite steht nur der erhöhte, kathederartige Stuhl („der Singstuhl") der Versammlung gegenüber. Im Hintergrunde, dem grossen Vorhang entlang, steht eine lange Bank für die Lehrlinge. — Walther verdriesslich über das Gespött der Knaben, hat sich auf die vordere Bank niedergelassen. Pogner ist mit Beckmesser im Gespräch aus der Sakristei aufgetreten. Die Lehrbuben harren ehrerbietig vor der hintern Bank stehend. Nur David stellt sich anfänglich am Eingang der Sakristei auf.)

Third Scene.

(*The arrangement of the stage is now thus completed; on the right stuffed benches are placed in a curve facing the centre. At the end of the benches, in the middle of the stage is the "Gemerk" (the marker's stage) which has been erected. On the left stands a high ecclesiastical chair (the "singing chair") opposite the benches. At the back in front of the great curtain stands a long bench for the pupils.— Walther, vexed with the boys' mocking, has seated himself on the front bench. Pogner has come from the sacristy in conversation with Beckmesser. The prentices stand waiting respectfully before the back bench. Only David takes his place at first by the sacristy door.*)

BECKM.

Doch wollt' ihr von dem Punkt nicht weichen, der mich_ich sag's_ be-denk-lich macht: kann
Yet will you not that point pass o-ver, where on, in truth, I'm doubtful still: if

Ev'-chens Wunsch den Wer - ber strei-chen, was nützt mir mei-ne Meis - ter-
E - va's whim may choose her lov-er, what booteth all my mas - ter

POG.

Ei sagt, ich mein', vor al - len Din - gen sollt' euch an dem ge - le - gen
But yet, me-seems your first be-gin-ning should be to find how well you

pracht?
skill?

poco cresc.

sein? Könnt ihr der Toch-ter Wunsch nicht zwin-gen, wie mög - tet ihr wohl um sie
stand; for if her heart you fail in win-ning, how then can you de - sire her

mf   *p*   *più p*

27327

84

POGN.

Rit - ter, dies geh' nun nach der Re - gel. Doch heut ist Freiung, ich schlag' euch
Wal - ther, such things by rule we set - tle. To-day is Tri - al, but have no

Kegel!
mettle!

p
f dim. -
P.

(Die Meistersinger sind nun alle angelangt, zu-
letzt auch Hans Sachs.)
(All the masters have now arrived, Hans Sachs last.)

vor, mir lei - hen die Meis - ter ein wil - lig Ohr.
fear; I gain from the mas - ters a will - ing ear.

p

VOGELGESANG.

HANS SACHS.
Sind wir bei-sammen?
Are all to - gether?

BECKM.
Gott grüss'euch, Meister!
God greet you, Masters!

NACHTIGAL.
Der Sachs ist ja da!
Yes, Sachs too, is here!

So ruft die
Let names be

poco a poco cresc. -
f

27327

86

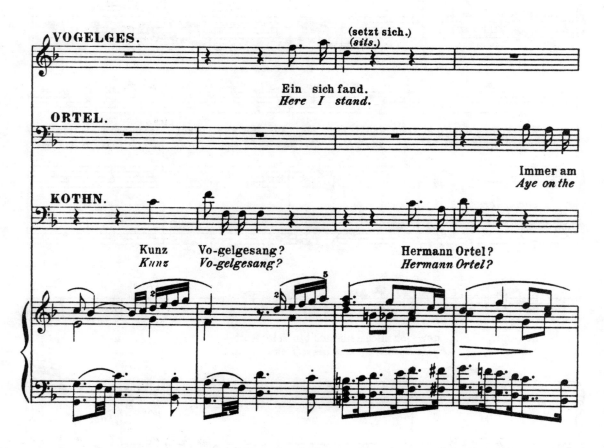

88

27327

DAVID. (vorlaut sich erhebend und auf Sachs zeigend.)
(rising and pointing to Sachs.)

Da steht er!
There stands he!

SACHS. (drohend zu David.)
(threateningly to David.)

(er setzt sich.)
(he sits.)

Juckt dir das Fell?__ Ver-zeiht, Meister!__ Sachs ist zur
Tin-gles thy face?__ For-give, Masters, Sachs is in

Sachs?
Sachs?

Stell!
place!

BECKMESSER.

(während er sich setzt.)
(as he takes his seat.)

Im-mer bei Sachs,__ dass den
E - ver by Sachs,__ so the

Six - tus Beckmesser?
Six - tus Beckmesser?

poco a poco cresc.__

(Sachs lacht.)
(Sachs laughs.)

Reim ich lern', von „blüh" und „wachs"!
rhyme I learn to "bloom and wax"!

Ul - rich Eiss - linger?
Ul - rich Eiss - linger?

dim.

27327

VOGELGES.

Wohl eh'r nach dem Fest?
The fest-i - val first.

BECKM.

Pressirt's den Herrn? Mein Stell' und
So pressing, sirs? To you I

KOTHN.

Beliebt's, wir schreiten zur Merkerwahl?
Shall we make choice of a marker now?

BECKM.

Amt lass' ich ihm gern.
gladly yield my place.

POGNER.

Nicht doch, ihr Meister, lasst das jetzt fort! Für wicht'gen Antrag bitt' ich um's
Not so; my Masters, let me be heard. For things of weight I ask for the

POGN.

Tanz im Lust-ge-lag, an fro-her Brust ge-bor-gen, ver-ges-sen sei-ner
dance a-mong the hay, with heart filled full of gladness, for-get-ting all his

Sor-gen, ein Je-der freut sich, wie er mag. Die Singschul' ernst im Kirchen-
sad-ness, let each re-joice as best he may. To raise the so-lemn chant on

chor die Meister selbst ver-tau-schen, mit Kling und Klang hinaus zum Thor, auf off'-ne
high, our singing school we bor-row: through gate and door, with shout and cry, to o-pen

Wie-se zieh'n sie vor, bei hel-len Fes-tes Rauschen das Volk sie las-sen
mea-dows all will hie: while there each one re-joi-ces, for ears unlearned our

27327

94

27327

POGN.

Statt, des bitt'ren Ta-dels ward' ich satt, dass nur auf Schacher und Geld, sein Merk der Bür-ger
cot, this bit-ter slander ceas-ed not__ that on-ly treasure and gold the burgher's dreams can

etwas lebhafter.

cresc.

f

stellt! Dass wir im wei - - ten deut - schen Reich die
hold! That in our em - - pire's spa - cious bounds our

Wieder ruhig.

dim.

p

Kunst ein - zig noch pfle - gen, d'ran dünkt ih - nen we - nig ge -
art we a - lone have tend - ed, me - seems, though 'tis lit - tle com -

P.

le - gen. Doch wie uns das zur Eh - re ge - reich', und dass mit ho - hem
mended, yet to our burgh - ers' hon - our re - dounds. And that in stead - fast

poco cresc.

P.

27327

POGN.

Muth wir schät - zen, was schön und gut, was
mood, we trea - sure the fair and good, the

werth die Kunst, und was sie gilt, das ward ich der Welt zu
pow'r of art and all its worth to that I would fain bear

zei-gen gewillt, d'rum hört, Meis - ter, die Gab', die als Preis bestimmt ich
witness on earth: this gift, then, I choose as prize: may ye Mas - ters deem it

hab'! Dem Sin - - - ger, der im
wise! To him whose song a-

POGN.

Kunst - ge - sang   vor   al -   lem Volk   den Preis er - rang,
mong the rest,   in o -   pen strife   ye judge   the best,

am Sankt Jo - han - nis - tag, sei er wer er auch mag,   dem geb'
on John the Baptist's day, be he who - e'er he may,   then will

ich,   ein Kunst - ge - wog'ner,   von Nü - renberg, Veit Pogner, mit all meinem
I,   as art's de - fender,   with all my goods sur - render the dear - est

Gut, wie's geh' und steh',   E - va, mein ein - zig Kind,   zur
trea - sure of my life   E - va, my on - ly child,   for

100

27327

102

ALT.
Pog - ner Veit!
Pog - ner's praise!

TENOR.
breit! Pog - ner Veit!
raise Pog-ner's praise!

VOGELGES.
sein?
be?

SACHS.
Sein Weib gäb' Mancher gern wohl
Some, be- - ing wed, would fain be

KOTHN.

P. +

SACHS.
d'rein!
free!

KOTHN.
Auf, le - dig' Mann! Jetzt macht euch
Up, sin - gle man! Do what you

f

P. P.

27327

104

POGNER.

zunft;
guild;
doch gilt's der Eh',
but maid-ens' hearts
so will's Ver-
may not be

p   *dolce*

nunft,
willed;
dass ob der Meis - - ter Rath
whom-e'er the Mas - - ters choose,
die
the

cresc. - - -

P.   ✠

KOTHN.

BECKM. (zu Kothner gewandt.)
(turning to Kothner.)

Versteh' ich
I un-der-

Dünkt euch das klug?
Doth that seem wise?

Braut den Aus - schlag hat.
bride may still re - fuse.

f   *p*

P.   ✠

27327

POGNER.

recht! / right!

Wen ihr Meis- ter den Preis zu- / If your judg- ment on one should

sprecht, die Maid ___ kann dem ver- / light who fails ___ to gain her

weh- ren, doch nie ei-nen and'-ren be- gehren. Ein / fa- vour, un- wed-ded she lives then for e- ver. A

poco riten. / rall.

Meis- ter-singer muss er sein, nur wen ihr krönt, / Mas- ter-singer must he be: he whom ye crown,

Etwas breiter. / Noch breiter werdend.

cresc.

27327

108

27327

VOGELGES.

tön'!
hood!

ZORN.

Kunst!
art!

MOSER u. EISSL.

tön'!
hood!

BECKM.

Tön'!
hood!

KOTHN.

Nein, Sachs! Ge-wiss, das hat keinen Sinn! Gäb't ihr dem Volk die Re-geln
Nay, Sachs! in-deed that plan has no sense. Ruled by the folk, all art goes

NACHTIG.

Tön'!
hood!

ORTEL.

Tön'!
hood!

stacc.

fp cresc. - *f*

P.

SACHS.

Vernehmt mich recht! Wie ihr doch thut! Ge - steht,
Nay hear a - right! Why chafe you so? Con - fess,

KOTHN.

hin?
hence?

stacc.

p tr *f* *sf* *p* cresc. -

P.

P.

SACHS.

ich kenn'_____ die Re - geln gut, und dass die
the rules_____ right well I know; and that the

Zunft die Re - geln be - wahr', be - müh' ich mich selbst schon man - ches
guild those rules well may guard, for ma - ny a year I've la - - boured

Jahr. Doch ein - mal im Jah - re fänd' ich's wei - se,
hard. sempre stacc. 'Twere well, when we meet each year to - geth - er,

dass man die Re - geln selbst pro - bir', ob in der Ge -
that we the rules them - selves should try, lest, soul - less and

27327

SACHS.

wohnheit trä-gemG'lei - se ihr Kraft und Le -
*tame in custom's teth - er, their force and life*____

- -ben nicht sich verlier'! Und ob ihr der Na -
should dwin - dle and die! And if on na - ture's

tur noch seid auf rech - ter Spur, das sagt euch nur,
road your feet have firm - ly trod, they know for sure

(Die Lehrbuben springen auf und reiben sich
die Hände.)
(*The prentices spring up and rub their hands.*)

wer nichts weiss von der Ta-bu-la - tur.
who nought know of the Ta-bu-la - ture.

SACHS (eifrig fortfahrend.)
(eagerly continuing.)

Drum mocht' es euch nie ge-reu-en, dass
Be-lieve me, you will not rue it, if

BECKM.

Hei! wie sich die Bu-ben freu-en!
Hey! see how the boys make merry!

cresc. — dim. —

jähr-lich am Sankt Jo-han-nis-fest, statt dass das Volk man kommen lässt, her-
once on Saint John's day ev'-ry year, trusting the crowd, ye should not fear to

Belebend im Zeitmass.

poco cresc. —

ab aus ho-her Meis-ter-wolk ihr selbst euch wen-det zu dem
leave your realm of mist and cloud and come your-selves to-wards the

piu cresc. —

Volk. Dem Vol-ke wollt ihr be-ha-gen, nun dächt' ich, läg' es nah': ihr
crowd. If ye the peo-ple would flat-ter, 'twould sure-ly help your aim, to

Etwas gemächlicher.

f dim. p

27327

114

27827

POGNER.

(Er wendet sich zu den Meistern.)
(He turns to the Masters.)

ich mein', ist schon neu; zu viel auf einmal brächte Reu! So
of-fer what is new; too much at one time we should rue! I

Mässiger.

frag' ich, ob den Meis - tern ge-fällt Gab' und Re - gel, so wie
ask then, if ye Mas - ters al-low prize and pro - mise as I

(Die Meister erheben sich beistimmend.)
(The Masters rise in assent.)

ich's ge - stellt? state them now.

BECKM.

SACHS.

Der Schuster weckt doch
The shoe-ma-ker a -

Mir ge - nügt der Jungfer Aus - schlag - stimm'.
Leave the maid-en free, and I give in.

27327

SACHS.

sein, soll Ev-chen ihm den Preis ver - leih'n.
prove, when E - va's heart bestows her love.

BECKM.

Als wie auch ich?— Gro-ber Ge-
Than I, you say? Ill-mannered

sell'
boor!

KOTHNER.

Begehrt wer Frei-ung, der komm'zur Stell'! Ist Jemand gemeld't, der Freiung be-
Who comes a - wooing? be not a-fraid! Is an-y one here who wishes to

gehrt?
wed?

POGNER.

Wohl, Meister, zur Ta-ges ordnung kehrt, und nehmt von mir Be-
Now Masters, the or-der of the day! And hear from me this

27327

120

27327

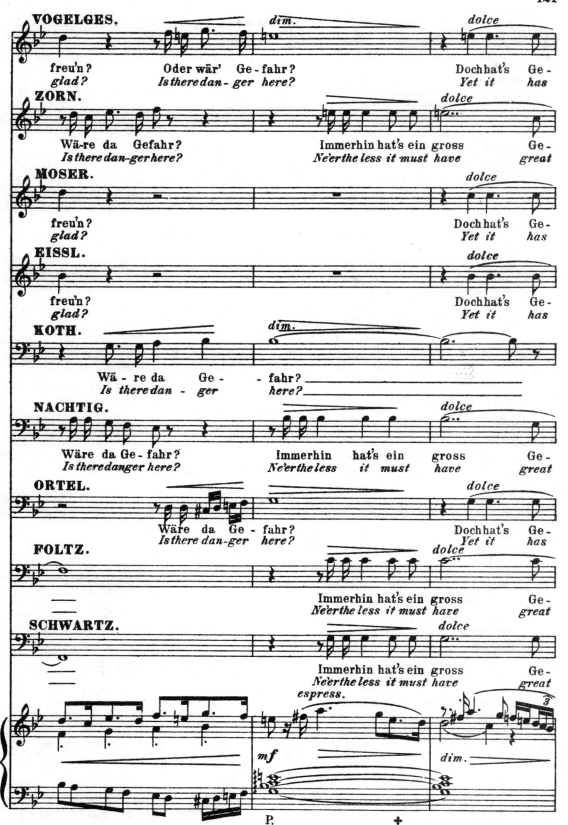

VOGELGES.
dim.
dolce
freu'n? Oder wär' Ge-fahr? Doch hat's Ge-
glad? Is there dan-ger here? Yet it has
ZORN.
dolce
Wä-re da Gefahr? Immerhin hat's ein gross Ge-
Is there dan-ger here? Ne'er the less it must have great
MOSER.
dolce
freu'n? Doch hat's Ge-
glad? Yet it has
EISSL.
dolce
freu'n? Doch hat's Ge-
glad? Yet it has
KOTH.
dim.
Wä - re da Ge- - fahr?
Is there dan - ger here?
NACHTIG.
dolce
Wäre da Ge-fahr? Immerhin hat's ein gross Ge-
Is there danger here? Ne'er the less it must have great
ORTEL.
dolce
Wäre da Ge - fahr? Doch hat's Ge-
Is there dan-ger here? Yet it has
FOLTZ.
dolce
Immerhin hat's ein gross Ge-
Ne'er the less it must have great
SCHWARTZ.
dolce
Immerhin hat's ein gross Ge-
Ne'er the less it must have great
espress.
mf
dim.
P.

122

VOGELGES.

wicht, dass Pog - ner für ihn spricht.
weight that Pog - ner for him speaks.

ZORN.

wicht, dass Meis - ter Pog - ner für ihn spricht.
weight that Mas - ter Pog - ner for him speaks.

MOSER.

wicht, dass Pog - ner für ihn spricht.
weight that Pog - ner for him speaks.

EISSL.

wicht, dass Pog - ner für ihn spricht.
weight that Pog - ner for him speaks.

KOTHN.

Soll uns der Jun - ker will -
Yet, if the knight is to

NACHTIG.

wicht, dass Meister Pog - ner für ihn spricht.
weight that Mas - ter Pog - ner for him speaks.

ORTEL.

wicht, dass Pog - ner für ihn spricht.
weight that Pog - ner for him speaks.

FOLTZ.

wicht, dass Meister Pog - ner für ihn spricht.
weight that Mas - ter Pog - ner for him speaks.

SCHWARTZ.

wicht.
weight.

p

dolce   p stacc.

P.   ✛   pp   P.   ✛

27827

KOTHNER.

kommen sein, zu-vor muss er wohl ver - nom-men sein.
join our guild, *he first must be tried* *and du-ly passed.*

POGNER.

Vernehmt mich wohl!
Mistake me not!

Wünsch' ich ihm Glück, nicht bleib' ich doch hin-ter der Re-gel zu-rück. Thut, Meister, die
Friend though he be, *yet I desire nought that the rules do not grant. Put, Masters, the*

p

P. P.

KOTHNER.

So mög' uns der Junker sa-gen: ist er frei und ehrlich ge-
So now let the knight first tell us: *are his birth and standing ap-*

Fragen.
questions.

poco cresc. *mf* *f* *p*

KOTHNER.

bo - ren?
proved?

POGNER.

Die Fra-ge gebt ver - loren, da ich euch selbst dess' Bürge steh', dass er aus
That question I will answer, for, as his sure-ty here I stand, that he is

frei' und ed - ler Eh': Von Stol - zing Wal - ther aus Franken-
free and no - bly born: the knight of Stol - zing in Franken-

land, nach Brief und Ur - kund mir wohl be-kannt. Als seines
land, by fame and let - ters to me well known. Sole living

Stammes letz-ter Spross verliess er neu - lich Hof und
sci - on of his race, of late he left his cas - tle

27327

schlossen ist, ob Herr und Bauer, hier nichts beschliesst: hier___ frägt sich's nach der Kunst al-
made of old, that lord and peasant a - like we hold: here___ nought is prized but art a-

lein, wer will ein Meister-sin-ger sein.
lone, in those who seek the Master's crown.

KOTHNER.

D'rum nun frag' ich zur Stell', welch'
Then his an - swer I claim: his

Meister's seid ihr Ge - sell'?
Mas-ter now let him name.

Noch mehr zurückhaltend.

WALTH.

Am stillen Herd in Winters-zeit, wann Burg und Hof mir ein-ge-
In snowbound hall by fire side, when prisoned fast at winter-

Mässig.

27827

128 SACHS.

Mei - ster.
mas - ter.

BECKM.

Doch lang' schon todt; wie lehrt' ihn der wohl der Re - geln Ge-
But long since dead; from him I won-der what rules could be

cresc. _ _ _ mf dim. p

KOTH.

Doch in wel - cher Schul' das Sin - - gen mocht' euch zu ler - nen ge-
In what school of art well found - ed, in all our laws were you

bot!
learned!

cresc.

WALTH.

Wann dann die Flur___ vom Frost be - freit,___ und
And when the fields___ the frost de - fied,___ and

lin - gen?
grounded?

sf p

wie - der - kehrt die Som - mers - zeit;___ was einst in
summer shone in ra - diant pride;___ what dur - ing

cresc. _ _ _ f dim. p p

P. + P +

27327

KOTH.

fort? Mich dünkt, der Jun - ker ist fehl___ am Ort.
halt? Me - thinks the knight is e'en now___ at fault.

p dolce

SACHS.

Das wird sich bäld - lich zei - gen: wenn rechte Kunst ihm ei - gen, und
We must not judge too light-ly if art has led him right-ly; if

gut___ er sie be - währt, was gilt's, wer sie ihm ge - lehrt?
well___ he sings by rule, what matters master or school?

cresc.

KOTH. (zu Walther.)
(*to Walther.*)

Seid ihr be - reit, ob euch ge - rieth___ mit neu - er
Are you prepared to show this throng, if you have

dim.

KOTH.

Find' ein Meisterlied, nach Dicht' und Weis' eur' ei-gen, zur Stunde jetzt zu
found a Mastersong with words and tune well mated, and by yourself cre-

WALTH

Was
The

zei - - gen?
a - - ted?

Win-ter-nacht, was Waldes-pracht, was Buch und Hain mich wie - sen, was
se-cret deep of winter's sleep, of woods in summer's glo - ry, the

Dichter-san - ges Wunder-macht mir heimlich wollt' er schlies - sen; was
hid-den word of book and bird, revealed in po - et's sto - ry; the

134

27327

136

27327

dem Gemerke zu.)
the "Gemerk".)

(Er verneigt sich gegen Walther.)
(He bows towards Walther.)

BECKM.

mal!
trow!

Wohl giebt's mit der Krei-de man-che Qual!
The chalk will be bu - sy, well I know!

cresc. — — — — f — mf

P.

Herr Rit - ter, wisst: Six-tus Beck-mes-ser Mer - ker
Sir Knight, give ear: Six-tus Beck-mes-ser mark - eth

p — poco cresc. — — — sf

ist; hier im Ge-merk' ver-rich-tet er still sein strenges
here: Here will he lurk and si-lent-ly do his cru-el

dol. — p
p — sf — dim. — tr — tr

Werk.
work.

Sie - ben Feh - ler giebt er euch
Se - ven faults he let - teth pass

p

P.

BECKM.

vor,
by,
die merkt er mit Krei - de dort an:— wenn er
with chalk they are marked on the slate:— but if

ü - ber sie-ben Feh - ler ver - lor,
more than seven faults he should spy,
dann
then,
ver -
Sir

(Er setzt sich im Gemerk.)
(He sits in the Gemerk.)

sang
Knight,
der Herr Rittersmann.
you have met your fate.
Gar fein er hört; doch dasser
His ears are keen; but, lest your

euch den Muth nicht stört,
soul, if he were seen,
säh't ihr ihm zu, so giebt er euch
should be dis - tressed, he leaves you at

27327

BECKM.

(Er streckt den Kopf, höhnisch freundlich nickend
(He puts out his head with a mocking friendly

Ruh', und schliesst sich gar hier ein,— lässt Gott euch be-foh-len
rest, and hides him-self a-way:— God grant you his grace to-

più p _pp_ _dim._

P.

KOTH. (winkt den Lehrbuben.)
(beckons to the prentices.)

heraus, und verschwindet hinter dem zugezogenen Vorhange des Gemerkes gänzlich.)
nod, and then disappears behind the drawn curtains of the "Gemerk.")

sein.
day.

più p _ppp_ _meno p_ _cresc._

u.c. t.c.

KOTH. (zu Walther.)
(to Walther.)

Was euch zum Lie-de Richt' und Schnur, ver-nehmt nun aus der Ta-bu-la-
These rules to make your foot-steps sure, now hear you from the ta-bu-la-

_p_ _cresc._

(Die Lehrbuben haben die an der Wand aufgehängte Tafel der "Leges Tabulaturae" herabgenommen,
(The prentices have taken down from the wall the board of the "Leges Tabulaturae" and

tur!
ture!

_f_ schwer _f_ _f_ _f_ _f_

sehr markirt.

27327

und halten sie Kothner vor; dieser liest daraus.)
hold it before Kothner who reads from it.)

KOTH.
(lesend)
(*reading*) *sehr markirt.*

Ein je - des Meister-gesanges   Bar stell' ordentlich ein Gemäs-se
A song hath "bars," as the Masters teach, which duly present a measure

dar   aus un - terschiedlichen Ge - sätzen, die Kei-ner soll ver-letz - - -
each: for this are sundry stanzas   needed, with laws that must be heed - - -

cresc.

en.
ed.

Ein Ge-sätz be -
In a stan - za

f stacc.

tr

steht aus zweenen Stollen, die glei-che Me - lo - dei ha-ben sollen; der Stoll'aus et-li-cher
strophes two are mated: one tune for these must then be cre-ated: each must to se-veral

p   cresc.   p   p

tr

27827

KOTH.

Vers' Ge - bänd, der Vers hat ei - nen Reim am End'
lines ex - tend, each line or verse a rhyme must end

Da-rauf er-folgt der Abgesang, der sei auch et-lich' Ver-se
There follows then the aftersong, which is se - veral verses

lang und hab' sein' be-sond'-re Me - lo-dei, als nicht im Stol-len zu fin-den
long. This al - so must have its me - lo-dy, the which must not in the strophe

sei
be

Der-
The

KOTH.

ruhig.

lei ___ Ge - mäs - ses meh - re   Ba - ren soll ein ___ jed'
songs ___ with "bars" of such a   mea - sure, as Mas - ter -

Meis - ter - lied be - wah - ren; und   wer ein neu - es Lied   ge - richt; das
songs we du - ly trea - sure. Of   se - quent notes as used   be - fore, our

ü - ber vier der Syl - ben nicht ein - greift in   and' - rer Meis - ter
rules al - low not more than four. Who sings a   song up - on   this

Weis',   dess'   Lied er - werb' sich   Meis - ter -
wise   shall   gain the   Mas - ter - sing - er's

144

27327

WALTH.

Hall von dan - nen flieht, von weit-her naht ein Schwel - len, das
reached its farth-est bound, when distant glens re - ply - -ing gave

mäch - tig nä - -her zieht. Es schwillt und schallt, es
back a might-y sound. The woods ere long are

tönt der Wald von hol - der Stimmen Ge-men-ge; nun
filled with song and sweet-ly clamour-ous voi-ces; now

laut und hell, schon nah' zur Stell; wie wächst der Schwall! Wie
loud and clear the sound draws near; the tu-mult swells like

27327

146

WALTH.

Glo - cken-hall er - tos't des Ju-bels Ge - drän-ge! Der
peal - ing bells, and ev' - ry creature re - joic - es! All

Wald,_____ wie bald ant - wor - tet er dem
heard_____ spring's word, and, an-swer-ing her com -

Ruf, der neu ihm Le - ben schuf___:
mand, that woke the sleep - ing land___,

stimm - te an das süs - se Len - zes -
raised on high the ten - der song___ of

Ossia.

27327

WALTH.(Man hört aus dem Gemerk unmuthige Seufzer des Merkers, und heftiges Anstreichen
mit der Kreide.— Auch Walther hat es gehört; nach kurzer Störung fährt er fort.)
(*From the "Gemerk" are heard Marker's sighs of illhumour and vigourous scratching
of the chalk; Walther hears it too, and, after a few moments of discomposure, continues.*)

lied.
spring.

In ei-ner Dornen-he-cken, von Neid und Gram ver-zehrt musst'
Deep hid in thorny co-ver, con-sumed by wrath and hate, when

er sich da ver-stecken, der Winter Grimm be-wehrt: von dür-rem Laub um-
now his reign is o-ver, old Winter lies in wait: in gloom of deep-est

rauscht, er lauert da und lauscht, wie er das fro-he Sin-gen zu
woods he cow-ers there and broods how all this singing's gladness his

27327

WALTH.

(Er steht vom Stuhle auf.)
(*He stands up.*)

Scha - den könn - te brin - gen!__
spite may turn to sad - ness:__

Doch fan - get an! So
But, now be - gin! My

rief es mir in der Brust,__ als noch ich von Lie - - be nicht
heart, too, heard the be - hest__ ere love yet was born__ in my

wusst! Da fühlt' ich's tief sich re - gen, als weckt' es mich aus dem
breast. Me-thought I woke from dream - ing; deep down my spi - rit was

150

WALTH.

Seuf - zer Heer in wil - dem Wonne __ Ge-wüh - le Die
tu - - mult rise and tell my passion __ of long - ing; I

Brust, wie bald ant - - wor - tet sie dem
heard spring's word and, answer - ing her be -

Ruf, __ der neu ihr Le - ben schuf; __
hest __ that woke my sleep - ing breast, __

stimmt nun an das heh - re Lie - - bes -
raised on high the glorious song __ of

154

27327

156

27327

SACHS (der vom Beginne an Walther mit wachsendem Ernst zugehört hat, schreitet vor.)
(*who from the first has listened to Walther with increasing earnestness, comes forward.*)

rum so komm' ich jetzt zum Schluss, dass den Jun-ker man zu End'
so, now hear my fin - al word, that the singer to the end

hö - ren muss.
must be heard.

Ver-
Now

BECKM.

Die Meister Zunft, die ganze Schul', ge-gen den Sachs da sind wir Null!
The Masters' guild and all the schools, set against Sachs are nought but fools!

hüt' es Gott, was ich be - gehr', dass das nicht nach den Geset - zen wär'!
God for - bid that I should claim to flout our laws or to thwart their aim!

Doch
But

da nun steht ge-schrieben: „Der Mer-ker wer - de so be - stellt, dass
they speak in this fashion: "The Marker shall be cho - sen so, that,

we - der Hass noch Lie-ben das Ur-theil trü - be, das er fällt."
free from hate and passion, he shall not swerve for friend or foe."

27327

P.

164

168

27827

174

27327

178

(Die Lehrbuben sind von der Bank aufgestanden und nähern sich dem Gemerk, um welches sie einen Ring schliessen und sich zum Reigen ordnen.)
(The Prentices have risen from the bench and form a ring round the "Gemerk," preparing to dance.)

188

(Walther verlässt mit einer stolz verächtlichen Gebärde den Stuhl und wendet sich rascn zum Fortgehen.-
Alles geht in grosser Aufregung auseinander; lustiger Tumult der Lehrbuben, welche sich des Gemerkes,
des Singstuhl's und der Meisterbänke bemächtigen, wodurch Gedränge und Durcheinander der nach dem
Ausgange sich wendenden Meister entsteht.)

(Walther, with a proudly contemptuous gesture leaves the chair and quickly turns to go. General excitement, merry tumult of the prentices who arm themselves with pieces of the Gemerk, the seat and the benches, causing confusion among the masters who are making for the door.)

189

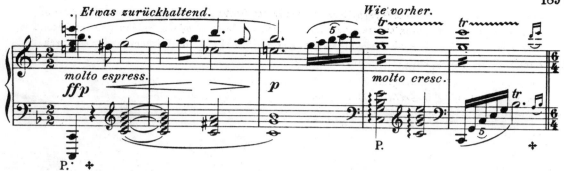

(Sachs, der allein im Vordergrunde geblieben, blickt noch gedankenvoll nach dem leeren Singstuhl; als die Lehrbuben auch diesen erfassen, und Sachs darob mit humoristisch unmuthiger Gebärde sich abwendet, fällt der Vorhang.)

(Sachs, who has remained alone in front, still gazes thoughtfully at the empty singer's chair. As the boys remove this, and Sachs turns away with a humourously indignant gesture, the curtain falls.)

Ende des ersten Aufzuges.
End of the first act.

Zweiter Aufzug.
Second Act.

Lebhaft, doch nicht zu schnell.

Der Vorhang geht auf. *The Curtain rises.*

Erste Scene.

Die Bühne stellt im Vordergrund eine Strasse im Längendurchschnitt dar, welche in der Mitte von einer schmalen Gasse, nach dem Hintergrunde zu krumm abbiegend, durchschnitten wird, so dass sich im Front zwei Eckhäuser darbieten, von denen das eine, reichere, rechts — das Haus Pogner's, das andere, einfachere, links das des Sachs ist. Vor Pogner's Haus eine Linde, vor dem Sachsen's ein Fliederbaum. — Heiterer Sommerabend; im Verlaufe der ersten Auftritte allmählich einbrechende Nacht. David ist darüber her, die Fensterläden nach der Gasse zu von aussen zu schliessen. Alle Lehrbuben thun das Gleiche bei andern Häusern.

First scene.

The front of the stage represents a street in longitudinal section, intersected in the middle by a narrow, crooked alley winding towards the back; of the two corner houses thus presented in front, the grander one on the right is Pogner's, the other, simpler one, is Sachs's. Before Pogner's house is a lime tree, before Sachs's an elder. A genial summer evening; in the course of the first scene night gradually falls. David is engaged in closing from without the shutters of the windows towards the alley. All the Prentices do the same for other houses.

194

195

27327

198

199

200

202

Zweite Scene.
(Pogner und Eva, wie vom Spazier-

Second scene.
(Pogner und Eva, returning from

(David und Sachs sind in die Werkstatt eingetreten
und gehen durch eine innere Thüre ab.)

SACHS. (David and Sachs have entered the workshop and go
off through an inner door.)

Leisten!
leave me!

Sehr gemächlich.

gange heimkehrend, — die Tochter leicht am Arme des Vaters eingehenkt, sind beide schweigsam die
Gasse heraufgekommen.)
a walk, have come in silence up the alley, the daughter lightly hanging on her father's arm.)

POGNER (durch eine Klinze im Fensterladen Sachsen's spähend.)
(peeping through a chink in Sachs's shutter.)

Lass seh'n,
We'll see

(David kommt mit Licht aus der Kammer, setzt sich
damit an den Werktisch am Fenster, und macht sich
über die Arbeit her.)
*(David comes from the inner room with a light, sits
at the work-bench by the window and works.)*

ob Meister Sachs zu Haus?   Gern spräch' ich ihn: trät' ich wohl ein?
if Mas-ter Sachs is there.   I'd speak with him: shall I go in?

EVA. (spähend.)
(peeping.)

Er scheint da-heim: kommt Licht her-aus.
He seems at home: his light shines out.

POGN.

(Er wendet sich ab.)
(He turns away.)

Thu' ich's? Zu was doch? Besser nein. Will Ei - ner Selt'nes
Shall I? Where for then? Better not. On ways un-wonted

Mässig.
pp cresc. sf dim. p

wagen, was liess' er sich dann sa-gen? War
moving, what man can brook re - proving? And

p dolce

er's nicht, der meint', ich ging' zu weit? Und, blieb ich nicht im Ge-
he 'twas who thought I went too far? Yet, though old customs not
espress.

cresc. f p

P. +

leise, war's nicht auf sei - ne Wei - se?__ Doch war's vielleicht auch
heeding, I followed so his leading? Yet still perchance some

cresc. - - dim. più p

206

27327

POGN.

Stadt, mit Bürgern und Ge-mei - nen, mit Zünften, Volk und hohem Rath vor
state, 'mid ac-cla-mations ring - ing, will come, with folk both small and great, to

dir sich soll ver-ei - nen, dass du den Preis, das ed - le Reis, er-
see thee crown our sing-ing, and thou as bride shalt stand beside the

thei - lest als Ge-mahl dem Meister dei - ner Wahl?
man who gains her voice, a Master of thy choice?

EVA.

Lieb' Vater, muss es ein Meister sein?
Dear father, Mas - ter, then, must he be?

POGN.

Hör'
But

27327

208

27327

sehr zart.

Mir löst er weich die Glie - der,   will, dass ich was sa - gen soll.—
Its sweet-ness weighs up - on   me;   *words from out my heart it calls.—*

pp

P.   P.   P.   P.

sehr leise.

Etwas gedehnter.
Erstes Zeitmass.

Was gilt's, was ich dir sa-gen kann? Bin gar ein
What boot such words as I can find within my

dolce   *pp*   *poco riten.*

P.

Lebhafter.   *Immer be_*

arm ein-fäl-tig' Mann!   Soll mir die Ar-beit nicht schmecken, gäb'st Freund, lieber mich
poor un-let-tered mind?   *When with my work I am wear-y, then, friend, let me go*

Lebhafter.   *Immer be_*

f   p   p   cresc. -

wegter.

frei, thät besser, das Le - - der zu stre - cken,   und liess' al-le Po-ë-te-
free; 'twere better with lea - - ther to plague me,   and let all this po-e-try

wegter.

f   sf   sf

27827

SACHS. (Er nimmt heftig und geräuschvoll die Schusterarbeit vor.)
(He begins to work abruptly and noisily.)

rei!
be!

Lebhaft.

(Er lässt wieder ab, lehnt sich von Neuem zurück,
(He leaves off again and leans back in thought.)

und sinnt nach.)

poco rall.

Sehr mässig.

Und doch, 'swill halt nicht gehn:—
And still, that strain I hear:—

ich fühl's,und kann's nicht ver - steh'n;— kann's nicht be-halten,— doch auch nicht ver-
I feel, yet no - thing is clear;— can-not for-get it,— nor can I en-

neu,— wie Vo - gel-sang im sü - ssen Mai!
born,— like song of birds on blithe May morn!

poco cresc. p dolce più p

Wer ihn hört, und wahn - be-thört sän - ge dem Vo - gel
If one heard, and mad - ly dared that song a-gain to

poco cresc.

nach, dem brächt' es Spott und Schmach.
sing; but scorn and shame'twould bring.

poco accel.

poco cresc. molto cresc.

Sehr breit.

Len - zes Ge-bot, die sü - sse Noth, die legt' es ihm in die
Spring-time's be-hest, with - in his breast, on heart and voice there was

Sehr breit.

dim.

27327

SACHS.

Brust:
laid:

nun sang er, wie er
then sang he as Nature

Mässig bewegt.

p dolce

P. ✛ P. ✛

musst';
bade;

und wie er musst', so konnt' er's,—
and to his need the pow-er

P. ✛ P. ✛ P. ✛

das merkt' ich ganz be-son-ders.
was grant-ed from her dow-er.

Etwas belebend.

cresc.—

rall.

sehr zart.

Dem Vo-gel, der heut' sang, dem war der
The bird who sang this morn, from Nature's

Mässig.

più p

pp

Schnabel hold   ge-wach-sen;   macht' er den Meistern bang, gar wohl ge-fiel   er doch Hans
self had learned his singing;   *Masters that song may scorn, for aye Hans Sachs will hear it*

Vierte Scene.
Fourth Scene.

(Eva ist auf die Strasse getreten, hat sich schüchtern der Werkstatt ge-
(Eva has come into the street and shyly approached Sachs's shop, and now
(Er nimmt mit heitrer Gelassenheit seine Arbeit vor.)
(He resumes his work with cheerful composure.)

Sach-sen!
ring-ing!

pp

nähert, und steht jetzt unvermerkt an der Thüre bei Sachs.)
stands unnoticed by Sachs's door.)

EVA.

Gut'n   A -   bend, Meister!   Noch so
Good   eve - ning, Master!   *Still a-*

più p

fleis - sig?   (Sachs fährt angenehm überrascht auf.)
work - ing?   *(Sachs starts in agreeable surprise.)*

Ei, Kind! Lieb'Evchen! Noch so   spät? Und doch,   warum so spät noch,
Ah child! Sweet Evchen! Still a -   *wake? Yet, why*   *so late awake, well*

poco rall.   **Mässig.**

f   *dim.*   *p dolce*

EVA.

Braut?
bride?

Ja! Weiss es die Stadt, Freund Sachs gu - te Gewähr dann
Yes, all the folk know! Friend Sachs good warrant no doubt, can

SACHS.

Ei, was! Das weiss die Stadt.
Ah well! All the folk know.

hat!   Ich dacht,   er wüsst mehr.   Ei,
show!   I thought   he knew more.   Ah,

Was soll ich wis - sen?
What should I know, then?

seht doch! Werd' ich's ihm sa-gen müssen?   Ich bin wohl recht dumm?
look now! Must I my secret show, then?   Am I, then, so dull?

Das sag' ich
I say not

Fä - den, da - mit ich dir die zie - ren Schuh' ge - fasst: heut'
stitch - ing, where - with for thee those dainty shoes I sewed: *shoes*

fass' ich die Schuh' mit dicht'ren Dräh - ten, da gilt's mit Pech für den derb'ren
now are in hand that call for pitch - ing, to fit a churl on his sto - ny

EVA.

Wer ist denn der? Wohl was recht's?
Who, then, is he? Some-one great?

Gast. Das mein' ich! Ein
road. *Aye tru - ly!* *A*

marcato

Mei - ster stolz auf Frei - er's Fuss; denkt mor - gen zu sie - gen ganz al -
Mas-ter proud who bold-ly woos, and hopes, too, to win, if honoured

EVA.

SACHS.

So nehmt nur
Then pitch in

lei- -nig: Herrn Beckmesser's Schuh' ich rich-ten muss.
du- -ly: for Beckmesser's feet I make these shoes.

tüchtig Pech da- zu: da kleb' er d'rin, und lass' mir Ruh'.
plenty let there be: may he stick there and leave me free.

Er hofft dich si-cher zu er-
His song he hopes will speed his

Wie so denn der?
A man like that!

sin-gen.
su-ing.

Ein Jung-ge-sell,—'s giebt de-ren we-nig dort zur Stell'!
A scan-ty band of batche-lors is here at hand!

27327

224

EVA. *sehr zart.*

Könnt's ei-nem Wittwer nicht ge - lin-gen?
Might not a wid-ow-er go woo-ing?

SACHS.

Mein Kind, der wär' zu alt für
My child, too old were he for

pp
pp *dolce*

P. +

Ei, was! zu alt?____ Hier gilt's der Kunst, wer sie ver-steht, der werb' um
Ah, what! too old?____ What wins is art; and all who sing, to woo are

dich.
thee.

dolce

3   3   2 4

P. +   P. +

mich.
free.

Nicht ich,
Not I,

Lieb' Ev - - chen machst mir blau-en Dunst?
Sweet Ev - - chen wouldst thou snare my heart?

espress.

dolcissimo

p

P. +   P. +

27327

EVA.

ihr seid's, ihr macht mir Flausen! Gesteht nur, dass ihr wandel-bar. Gott weiss, wer euch
you 'tis— you that are cunning! Your falseness you dare not de-ny. God now knows on

jetzt im Her-zen mag hau-sen! Glaubt' ich mich doch d'rin so man - ches
whom your fan-cy is running! This man-y a year I dreamed 'twas

poco cresc.

p

Jahr.
I.

(sehr zart.)
(very tenderly.)

Ich seh', 'swar nur, weil ihr
I see why 'twas; you were

SACHS.

Wohl, da ich dich gern auf den Ar-men trug?
Because in my arms thou hast often lain?

dim.

kin-der-los. (weich)
childless then. (softly)

Hatt' einst ein Weib,— und Kin-der ge-
Yet once were wife — and children my

pp

P. P. 27327 P.

Etwas lebhafter.

EVA.

Ein Rit - ter? Mein, sagt!—
A knight'twas? *Ah me!—*

SACHS.

Ein Jun - ker, Kind, gar un-be - lehrt.
A knight, my child, and all un - taught.

Und ward er ge-freit?
Then say, did he pass?

Nicht's da, mein Kind! 'sgab gar viel
Not so, my child! much strife there

So sagt,— er - zählt,— wie ging es
Then tell,— re - late;— how did it

Streit.
was.

EVA.

kein Mit-tel gäb's, das ihm ge - dieh'?
to give him aid, was there no way?

Sang er so schlecht, so feh - lervoll, dass
Was, then, his song of fault so full that

nichts mehr zum Mei-ster ihm hel-fen soll?
none might de - fend him in all your school?

SACHS.

Immer breiter im Zeitmass.

Mein Kind, für den ist Al - les ver - lo - ren, und
My child, the man who meets such dis - as - ter, no

sempre rall.

Mei - ster wird der in kei-nem Land;
Mas - ter will be in a - ny land.

denn wer als Mei - ster ge -
Who-e'er is born as a

sehr breit.

MAGD.

(vernehmlicher rufend.)
(calling more audibly.)

Der Va - ter ver-
Thy father has

so - ren, der hat un-ter Mei-stern den schlimmsten Stand.
mas - ter, finds e - ver with Mas-ters the low - est stand.

wieder belebend. schnell belebend. so lebhaft wie vorher.

27327

SACHS.

Mag er durch die Welt sich ranfen;
Let the bustling world a-wake him.
was wir er - lernt mit Noth und
Shall he then rob and leave us

Müh', _____ da - bei lasst uns in Ruh' ver-schnau-fen:
bare_____ of what by la - bour we have won us?

Etwas breit.

hier renn' er uns nichts über'n Hau - fen; sein Glück ihm an-ders wo er -
Here ne-ver shall he over-run us: let for-tune greet him o-ther

EVA.

(Sie erhebt sich zornig.)
(She rises angrily.)

Ja! an - - ders wo
Aye, o - - ther-where

blüh'!
where!

Lebhaft.

sehr feurig.

EVA.

soll's — ihm er - blüh'n, alsbaleuch garstgen neid'- schen
shall — for-tune greet! whate'er an envious churl- ish

Mannsen, — wo warm die Her - zen noch er-
man says, — where hearts with lov - ing ar - dour

glü - hen, trotz al-len tück'- schen Meis-ter Han - sen! Gleich, Le-ne,
beat — in spite of cross-grained Mas - ter Hans-es! Yes, Le-ne,

(zu Magdalene.)
(to Magdalene.)

gleich! Ich kom-me schon! Was trüg' ich hier für Trost da-von? Da riecht's nach
yes! At once I'll come, and bet-ter comfort seek at home. Lest smell of

27327

236

27827

238

MAGD. (zieht die sich sträubende Eva am Arm die Stufen zur Thür hinauf.)
(pulls the resisting Eva up the steps to the house.)

Zeit.
deed.

Hörst du's?
Hear'st thou?

Komm'!
Come!

Dein Ritter ist
thy knight is not

Fünfte Scene.
Fifth Scene.

EVA.

(Sie erblickt Walther.)
(She sees Walther.)

(Walther ist die Gasse heraufgekommen; jetzt biegt er um die Ecke herum.)
(Walther has come up the alley; he now turns the corner.)

Da
There

weit!
there.

Ziemlich lebhaft.

p

molto cresc.

P.

(Sie reisst sich von Magdalene los, und stürzt Walther auf die Strasse entgegen.)
(She tears herself away from Magdalene, and rushes towards Walther.)

ist er!
is he!

(Sie geht eilig in das Haus.)
(She goes hastily into the house,

Da haben wir's!
Now wit a-lone

Nun heisst's:
can help

ge - scheit!
us out!

ff

f

f

P.

246

27327

WALTH.

dich nun be-schwör' ich, komm' und
what-e'er be-fall me, fly with

folg' mir hin-aus!
me, then, to-night!

Nichtssteht zu hoffen; keine Wahl ist offen! Ueberall Meister, wie bö-se
Hope is bereft us; not a choice is left us, nought but dis-asters! Ev'ry-where

Lebhaft.
sehr gestossen.

Geister, seh' ich sich rotten, mich zu ver-spot - - ten:
Masters! There they are flocking round me and mock - - ing:

WALTH.

mit den Ge - wer - ken,
ev'-ry where judges,
aus den Ge - mer - ken, aus al - len E - cken,
markers with grudges; out from all al - leys

auf allen Flecken, seh' ich zu Haufen Meister nur laufen, mit höhnendem Nicken frech auf dich
making their sallies, crowds of them hustling. Masters are bustling; in jeering gri-maces twist - ing their

blicken, in Krei-sen und Rin-geln dich um - zingeln, näselnd und
faces; in circles a - bout thee, so to flout thee; snuffling and

krei - schend zur Braut dich hei - schend, als Meis-terbuh - le auf dem
screech - ing, thy hand be - seech - ing; as Mas - ters' play - thing on the

WALTH.

Sin - gestuh - - le zit - ternd und be - - bend,
throne they place thee, trem - bling and quak - - -ing,

hoch dich er - he - - bend! Und ich er - -
there to dis - grace thee! And I must

trüg' es. sollt' es nicht wa - gen, g'rad' aus tüch - tig
bear it, tame - ly at - tend them, dare not fall on

(Man hört den starken Ruf
eines Nachtwächterhornes.)
*(The loud horn of the Night-
warder is heard.)* (Walther hat mit
(Schrei.) *(Walther has laid*
(Cry.)

d'rein zu schla - - - gen? Ha!
them and rend - - - them? Ha!

NACHTWÄCHTER (auf dem Stierhorne.)
NIGHT-WATCHMAN *(on the cow-horn.)*

EVA.

Von hinnen! Von hinnen! O wä-ren wir schon fort!
Away now! Away now! Oh, would that we were gone!

WALTH.

Hier durch die Gasse, dort finden wir vor dem
Here through the alley, then. Ready, without the

pp

molto cresc. - - - -

P.

(Als sich Beide wenden, um in die Gasse einzubiegen, lässt Sachs,
nachdem er die Lampe hinter eine Glaskugel gestellt, durch die ganz
wieder geöffnete Ladenthüre einen grellen Lichtschein quer über
die Strasse fallen, so dass Eva und Walther sich plötzlich hellbe-
leuchtet sehen.)

(As they both turn to go into the alley, Sachs, after placing his lamp be-
hind a glass globe, lets a bright beam of light fall across the alley
through the opened shutter so that Eva and Walther suddenly find
themselves clearly illuminated.)

(Walther hastig zurückziehend.)
(hastily drawing Walther back.)

EVA.   **Ziemlich belebt.**

O weh! Der Schuster! _   Wenn der uns
A-las! The cobbler. _   *If he should*

Thor   Knecht und Rosse   vor.
gate, squire and horses   *wait.*

NACHTW.

(auf dem Horn, entfernt.)
(on the horn, at a distance.)

p

Ziemlich belebt.

f   **p**   **sf**   **p**

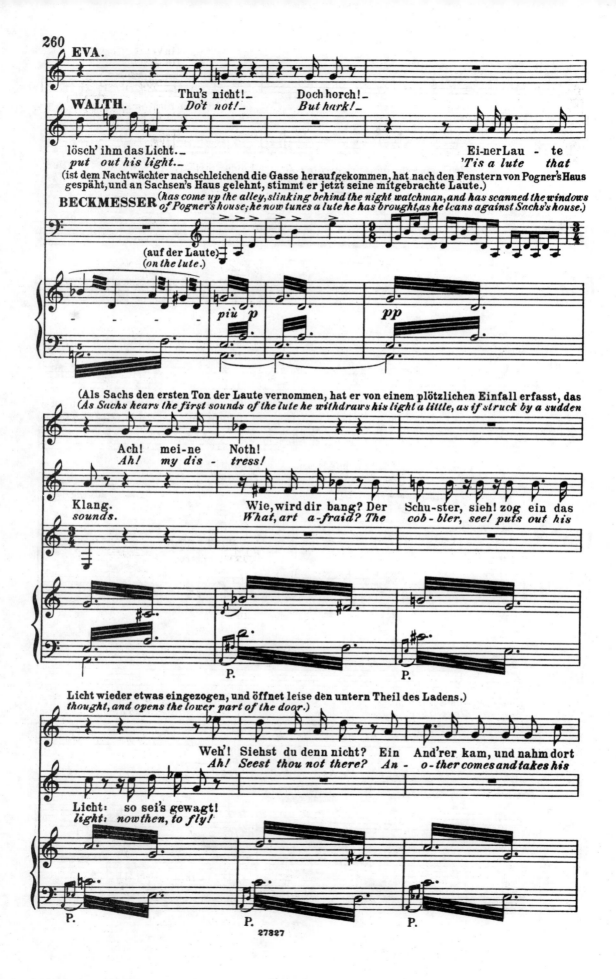

261

262

EVA.

Va-ter wecken? Er singt ein Lied, dann zieht er ab.— Lass'
wake my father? He'll sing a song, and leave us then.— Here

più p

poco marcato

dort uns im Gebüsch ver-stecken!— Was mit den Männern ich
let us in the ar-bour hide us!— What trou-ble e-ver I

BECKM. (eifrig nach dem Fenster lugend, klimpert voll Ungeduld heftig auf der Laute. Als er sich
endlich auch zum Singen rüstet, schlägt Sachs sehr stark mit dem Hammer auf den Lei-
sten, nach dem er soeben das Licht wieder hell auf die Stras-
se hat fallen lassen.)

*(eagerly gazing at the window, strums loudly on the lute, in
impatience. When he at length prepares to sing, Sachs strikes
a heavy blow with his hammer on the last, after turning the
light of his lamp full on the street again.)*

(auf der Laute.)
(on the lute.)

più p

P.

P.

(Sie zieht Walther hinter das Gebüsch auf die Bank unter der Linde.)
(She draws Walther on to the seat behind the foliage under the lime tree.)

EVA. **Kräftig bewegt.**

Müh' doch hab'!
have with men!

(sehr stark.)
(very loud.)

SACHS.

BECKM. (auf der Laute.)
(on the lute.)

Je - rum!
Je - rum!

Kräftig bewegt.

pp

ff f geräuschvoll

P. P.

P.

27327

263

27827

SACHS.

schu ihr Schmerz der har - te Kies an ih - rem Fuss, dem blo -
toil-ing o'er the sto - ny waste, her feet were sore tor - ment-

- sen.
- *ed.*

Das
There-

BECKM.

Was fällt dem groben Schu-ster ein?
What plan is in the cob-bler's head?

EVA.

(flüsternd zu Walther.)
(whispering to Walther.)

Ich hört es schon; 'sgeht nicht auf
I heard it well; but 'tis not

WALTH. (flüsternd zu Eva.)
(whispering to Eva.)

Was heisst das Lied? Wie nennt er dich?
What means the song? Thy name I hear.

jammer-te den Herrn,   ihr Füsschen   hatt' er gern: und
at the Lord was moved,   her ten-der   feet he loved: some

dim.   p   p

WALTH. (wie vorher.) (as before.)

Uns o-der dem Merker, wem spielt er den Streich?
Is't we or the Marker? At whom does he jeer?

SACHS.

hast du am Ge-wis- -sen, dass ob der Füss' am
caused thee bit-ter ru- -ing, that now the feet of

EVA (wie vorher.) (as before.)

Ich fürcht', uns drei-en gilt er gleich.
His song re-proves all three, I fear.

Men-schen-leib jetzt En-gel schu-stern müs- - - - - -
mor-tal men the an-gels must be shoe- - - - - -

O Weh', der Pein! Mir ahnt nichts
Ah woe is me! I fear some

- -sen!
- -ing!

Bliebst du im Pa-ra-
Stones were not e-ver

strei - che Pech! Wär' ich nicht fein ein
spend my time! Were I not, too, an

En - gel rein, Teu - fel möch - te Schu - -
an - gel true, dev - ils might make shoes

- - ster sein! Je - - - Je - -
for you! Je - -

(sich unterbrechend.)
(interrupting himself.)

BECKM. (drohend auf Sachs zufahrend.)
(coming threateningly towards Sachs.)

Gleich hö - ret auf! Spielt ihr mir Streich'?
Come to an end! What is this trick?

Bleibt ihr Tag's und Nacht's euch gleich?
Night and day are you the same?

272 SACHS.

SACHS.

drüs - sen! Die Kunst-werk', die ein Schus - ter schuf, sie
ge - -ther! The world con - temns the cob - bler's art and

tritt die Welt mit Füs - - - - - -
treads up - on his lea - - - - - -

- - -sen!
- - -ther!

SACHS.

(weich.) *langsam.*

Gäb' nicht ein En- gel Trost, der glei-chesWerk er- los't, und rief mich oft in's
Were not an an- gel there, to charm a - way my care, to Pa-ra- dise oft

poco rall.

Pa - ra - dies, wie ich da Schuh' und Stie- fel liess! Doch
call-ing me, I soon would let my cob- bling be! But

Pa - ra - dies, wie ich da Schuh' und Stie- fel liess! Doch
call-ing me, I soon would let my cob- bling be! But

wenn mich der im Him-mel hält, dann liegt zu Füs- sen
when en - throned in Heaven's seat, the world doth lie be -

mir die Welt, und bin in Ruh' Hans Sachs, ein Schuh-
neath my feet; then, born a-new, I am a shoe-

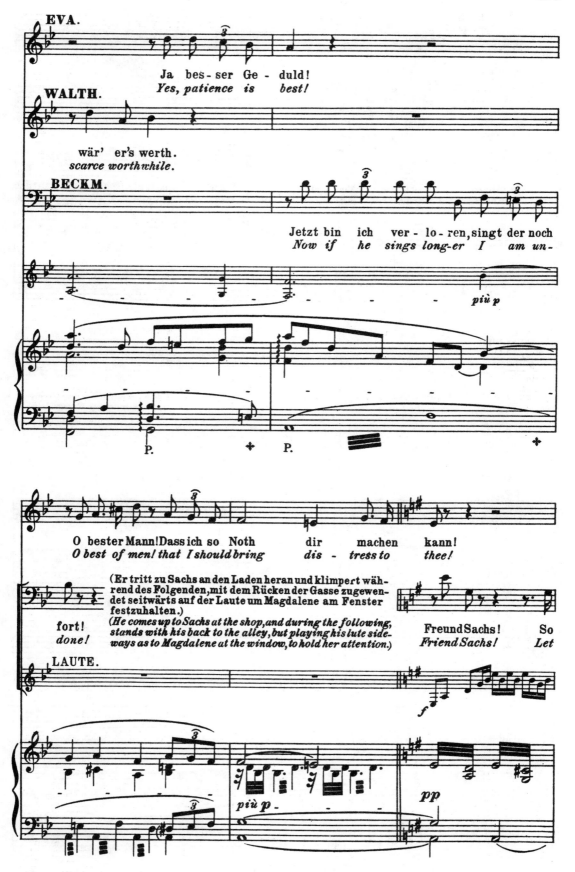

278

SACHS.

noch gedehnter.

fassen? Mag mich nicht wie-der schel-ten las-sen. Seit sich der
catch me? Not a - gain will I let you teach me how, since the

Schus-ter dünkt Po - et___ gar ü - bel es um eu'r
cob - bler po - et has been, such shoes he makes as ne'er

Allmählich etwas lebhafter.

Schuhwerk steht: ich seh', wie's schlappt und ü - ber - all
yet were seen: un-sound through-out, they flap all a-

klappt; d'rum lass' ich Vers und Reim'___ gar bil - lig
bout! Writ - ing of songs, I swear,___ for you I

281

BECKM.

Herz.   Vom Volk _____ seid ihr ge-ehrt,   auch der Pog-ne-rin seid ihr
breast.   *The folk _____ will feel your spell,*   *and the maiden, too, loves you*

LAUTE.

(wie vorher.)
(as before.)

werth: will ich vor al-ler Welt   nun mor-gen um die werben,   sagt!___
well: *if I to-morrow came,*   *to win the people's favour,*   *were't*

könnt's mich nicht verderben, wenn mein Lied ihm nicht gefällt? D'rum hört mich ruhig an, und
not a vain endeavour, if my song Hans Sachs should blame? Now listen to my song, and

(wie vorher.)
(as before.)

284

27827

286

27327

BECKM. accel.

Sachs, nie wird er je zum Mer - ker be-stellt.
Sachs, ne - ver shall you as Mark - er be named. (Er klimpert in höchster Wuth.)
(He plays in intense fury.)

LAUTE.

ff

Allmählich zurückhaltend.

cresc. sf

Der Teufel hol's!
Ill-mannered hound!

SACHS. (der ihm ruhig und aufmerksam zugehört hat.)
(who has listened to him quietly and attentively.)

War das eu'r Lied?
Was that your song?

Mässig.

Zwar wenig
The rules were

più p

P. stacc. ⊕

Wollt ihr mich hören?
Will you not hear me?

Re - gel, dochklang's recht stolz.
lack - ing, but brave the sound.

In Got - tes
For Heaven's

cresc.

sf p cresc.

f

P. ⊕ 27327 P. ⊕ P. ⊕

BECKM.

SACHS.

Namen, singt zu: ich schlag' auf die Sohl' die Rahmen.
sake, then, sing you; while shoes for your feet I make, then.

Doch schweigt ihr still?
But, you'll keep still?

Ei, sin-get
Oh, sing you

ihr, die Ar - beit, schaut, fördert's auch mir.
on, my cob-bling, too, is not yet done.

Das verfluchte
That accursed

Klop-fen wollt ihr doch lassen?
knocking pass-es all bearing!

Wie sollt' ich die Sohl' euch richtig
But must not your shoes be fit for

27327

BECKM.

SACHS. Was? Ihr wollt klopfen, und ich soll sin-gen?
What! must I sing, then, while you beat leather?

fas-sen? Euch muss das
wearing? Both song and

Ich mag keine Schuh'!
I want not the shoes!

Lied, mir der Schuh ge - lin - gen.
shoe must ad - vance to - geth - er.

SACHS. Das sagt ihr jetzt: in der Singschul' ihr mir's dann wieder ver-
You say so now: but to - mor - row morn you will blame me, I

poco rallent.

setzt. Doch hört! Viel - leicht sich's rich-ten lässt; zwei-
trow. Yet hear! Per - chance it may be done; two

Mässig.

27327

290

SACHS.

ei - nig geht der Mensch am best'. Darf ich die
comrades bet - ter speed than one. Al - though my.

Ar - beit nicht ent - fer - nen, die Kunst des Mer - ker's möcht' ich er -
work brooks no de - ni - al, in Mark - er's craft now give me a

ler - nen; da - rin kommt euch___ nun Kei - ner
tri - al. In that you have___ no peer, 'tis

gleich: ich lern' sie nie, wenn nicht von euch.
true: how learn the art if not from you?

27327

292

27327

294

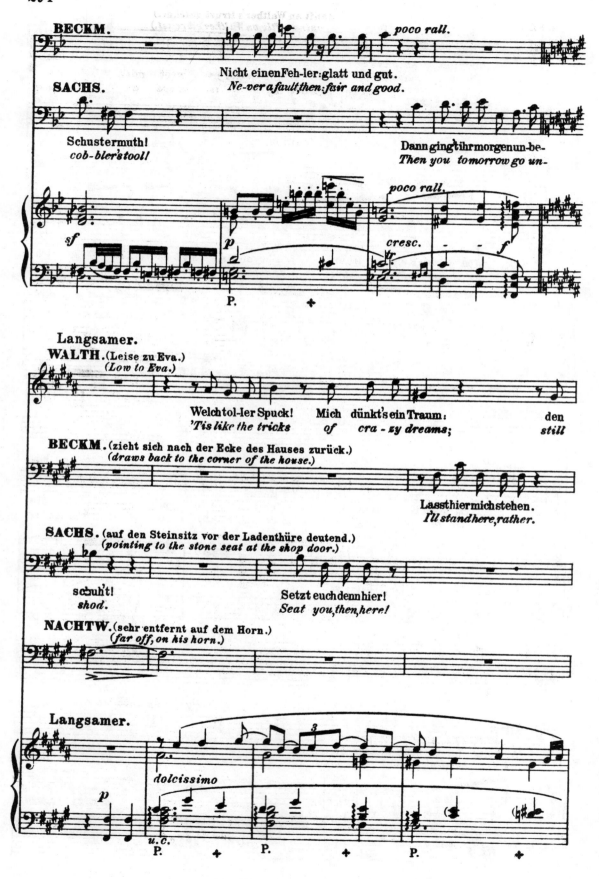

298

27327

BECKM.

thut;
true;

da fasst mein Herz sich ei - nen gu - ten und fri - schen
and wakes in me a gay, light heart and a courage

LAUTE.

(ad lib.)

Muth:
new.

da denk' ich nicht an Ster - ben, lie-ber an Wer -
I think not now of dy - ing; rather of try -

SACHS.

(schlägt)
(strikes)

ben um jung Mägdelein's Hand.
ing to win a young maid's hand.

Warum wohl al - ler Ta-ge schönster mag dieser
Why think I of this day, it o - ther days doth ex-

(schlägt)
(strikes)

(schlägt)
(strikes)

27327

310

27327

311

27327

312

27327

314

DAV.

Nun warte, du kriegst's!
Wait till I be-gin!

Dir streich ich das
I'll polish your

BECKM.

(Er verschnauft sich.)
(out of breath.)

gen um jung Mägdelein's Hand.
rors who seeks for a maid's love.

Ein Junggesell ____ trug ich mein Fell, ____
For, by the muse, ____ my skin I'd lose, ____

SACHS.

____ - - - der.
____ *it.*

Nun lauft in Ruh':
Now take your road;

habt
you're

VOGELG.

Gebt Ruhe hier!
Keep quiet, there!

ZORN.

Schla-fen'szeit.
sleep-ing time.

Gebt Ruhe hier!
Keep quiet, there!

KOTH.

'Sist Schlafen'szeit.
'Tis sleeping time.

NACHT.

'Sist Schla - - - fen's-zeit.
'Tis sleep - - - ing time.

ORTEL.

Ist das erlaubt, so spät zur Nacht?
Is that allowed so late at night?

FOLTZ.

Schlafen'szeit.
sleeping time.

NACHBARN.
NEIGHBOURS.

poco f (Mit Holzbläsern in gestossenen Triolen, wie früher.) *poco cresc.*

poco f p Melodie f poco cresc.

P. + P.

27827

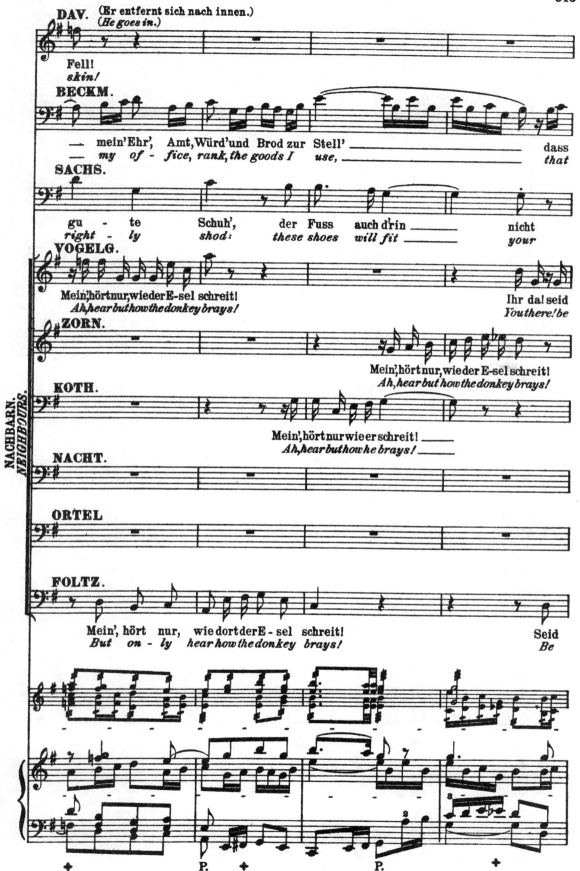

27327

Siebente Scene.
Seventh Scene.

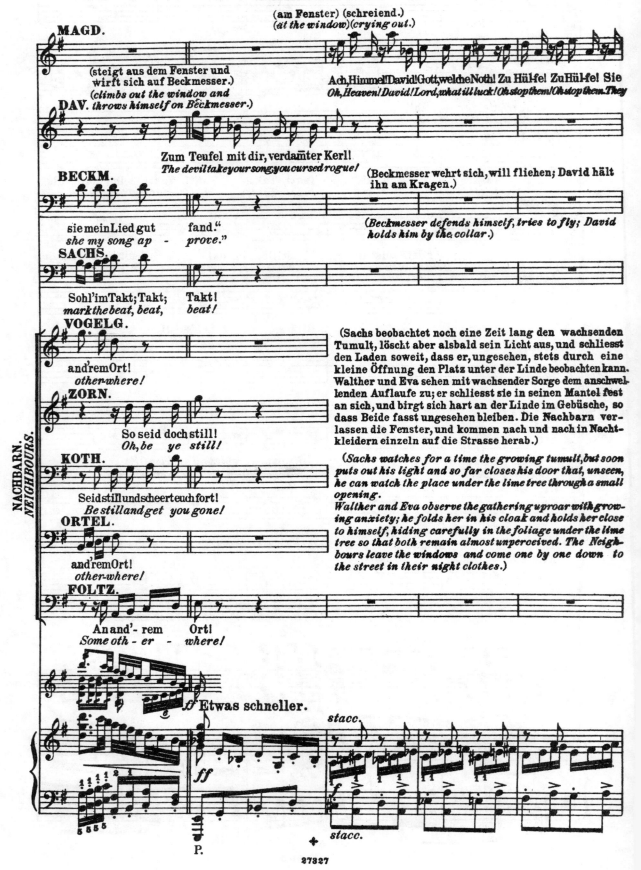

(Sachs beobachtet noch eine Zeit lang den wachsenden Tumult, löscht aber alsbald sein Licht aus, und schliesst den Laden soweit, dass er, ungesehen, stets durch eine kleine Öffnung den Platz unter der Linde beobachten kann. Walther und Eva sehen mit wachsender Sorge dem anschwellenden Auflaufe zu; er schliesst sie in seinen Mantel fest an sich, und birgt sich hart an der Linde im Gebüsche, so dass Beide fasst ungesehen bleiben. Die Nachbarn verlassen die Fenster, und kommen nach und nach in Nachtkleidern einzeln auf die Strasse herab.)

(Sachs watches for a time the growing tumult, but soon puts out his light and so far closes his door that, unseen, he can watch the place under the lime tree through a small opening.
Walther and Eva observe the gathering uproar with growing anxiety; he folds her in his cloak and holds her close to himself, hiding carefully in the foliage under the lime tree so that both remain almost unperceived. The Neighbours leave the windows and come one by one down to the street in their night clothes.)

319

27327

27327

336

27827

337

(Sogleich mit dem Eintritte des Nachtwächterhornes(¾ Takt) haben die Frauen aus allen Fenstern starke Güsse von Wasser aus Kannen, Krügen und Becken auf die Streitenden hinabstürzen zu lassen; dies, mit dem besonders starken Tönen des Hornes zugleich, wirkt auf Alle mit einem panischen Schrecken. Nachbarn, Lehrbuben, Gesellen und Meister suchen in eiliger Flucht nach allen Seiten hin das Weite, so dass die Bühne sehr bald gänzlich leer wird; die Hausthüren werden hastig geschlossen; auch die Nachbarinnen verschwinden von den Fenstern, welche sie zuschlagen.)

(At the moment of the night-warder's entrance (¾ time) the women pour out of all windows, from cans, jugs and basins, copious streams of water down on to the fighters; this, together with the very loud tone of the horn produces a general panic. Neighbours, Prentices, Journeymen and Masters fly in all directions, so that the stage very soon becomes empty. The women also disappear and close the windows.)

27327

SACHS.(die halb ohnmächtige Eva die Treppe hinaufstossend.)
(pushing the almost fainting Eva up the steps.)

(Pogner empfängt Eva,und zieht sie am Arm
in das Haus.Sachs,mit dem Knieriemen David eines überhauend,und mit einem Fusstritt
ihn voran in den Laden stossend,zieht Walther,den er mit der andern Hand fest gefasst
hält,gewaltsam schnell ebenfalls mit sich
hinein,und schliesst sogleich fest hinter sich
zu. Beckmesser,durch Sachs von David be-
freit,sucht sich,jämmerlich zerschlagen,
eilig durch die Menge zu flüchten.)
(Pogner receives Eva,and pulls her by the
arm into the house.Sachs giving David a
stroke with his stirrup and,sending him
into the shop by a kick,draws Walther,whom
he has seized with his other hand,quickly
and forcibly with him into the house which
he immediately closes behind him. Beck-
messer,freed from David by Sachs,woe-
fully battered,hastily tries to escape through
the crowd.)

In's Haus, Jungfer Le-ne!
Go in, Mistress Le-ne!

NACHTW.

Als die Strasse und Gasse leer geworden,und alle Häuser ge-
When the street and alley are empty and all the houses are

Allmählich ruhiger im
Zeitmass.

schlossen sind, betritt der Nachtwächter im Vordergrunde rechts die Bühne, reibt sich die Augen, sieht
closed, the night-warder enters in front R, rubs his eyes, looks around in surprise, shakes his head

piu dim.

sich verwundert um, schüttelt den Kopf, und stimmt mit leise bebender Stimme den Ruf an.)
and sings his verse with a tremulous voice.)

NACHTWÄCHTER.

Hört, ihr Leut', und lasst euch sa - gen, die Glock' hat
Hear, all folk, the war-der's dit - ty; e - le - ven

pp

el - - fe ge - schla-gen: be-wahrt euch vor Ge-spenstern und
strikes_____ in our ci - ty: de-fend yourselves from spectre and

immer mehr abnehmend.

Spuck, dass kein bö - ser Geist eu'r Seel' be - ruck'!
sprite, that no e - vil imp your souls af - fright!

NACHTW.

(auf dem Horn.)
(on the horn.)

(Der
(The

Lobet Gott, den Herrn!
Praiseye God the Lord!

ff ——————— **p**

Sehr ruhig im Zeitmass.

pp

ppp

u. c.

Vollmond tritt hervor, und scheint hell in die Gasse hinein; der Nachtwächter schreitet langsam
full moon comes out, and shines brightly into the alley, down which the Night-warder slowly
staccatissimo

dieselbe hinab.)
walks.)

(Als hier der Nachtwächter um die Ecke biegt, fällt der Vorhang schnell, genau mit dem letzten Takte.)
(As the Night-warder turns the corner, the curtain falls quickly exactly with the last chord.)

27327

Dritter Aufzug.
Third Act.

Erste Scene.

In Sachsens Werkstatt. *(Kurzer Raum.)* Im Hintergrunde die halbgeöffnete Ladenthüre,nach der Strasse führend. Rechts zur Seite eine Kammerthüre. Links das nach der Gasse gehende Fenster, mit Blumenstöcken davor, zur Seite ein Werktisch. Sachs sitzt auf einem grossen Lehnstuhle an diesem Fenster, durch welches die Morgensonne hell auf ihn hereinscheint; er hat vor sich auf dem Schoosse einen grossen Folianten, und ist im Lesen vertieft.

First Scene.

In Sachs's workshop (Front scene.) *At back the half open door leading to street. On the right side a chamber door. On the left a window looking on the alley, with flowers before it; on the same side a work bench. Sachs sits in a large arm chair at this window, through which the morning sun shines brightly upon him: he has a large folio on his lap and is arsorbed in reading it.*

(David zeigt sich von der Strasse kommend unter der Ladenthüre; er lugt herein und da er Sachs gewahrt, fährt er zurück.)
(David is seen coming from the street. He peeps in and on seeing Sachs starts back.)

(Er versichert sich aber, dass Sachs ihn nicht bemerkt, schlüpft herein, stellt seinen mitgebrachten Korb auf den hinteren Werktisch beim Laden, und untersucht seinen Inhalt; er holt Blumen *(He is rearsured as Sachs does not see him and slips in, places a basket he has brought on the work bench at back by the door, and examines its contents; he takes out flowers and*

und Bänder hervor, kramt sie auf dem Tische aus, und findet endlich auf dem Grunde eine Wurst und einen *ribbons, lays them out on the table and at last finds at the bottom a sausage and a cake; he prepares to*

Kuchen; er lässt sich an, diese zu verzehren, als Sachs, der ihn fortwährend nicht beachtet, mit starkem Geräusch eines der grossen Blätter des Folianten umwendet.)
eat thee when Sacks who has not taken notic of him, noisily turns over a leaf of the folio.)

DAVID (fährt zusammen, verbirgt das Essen, und wendet sich zurück.)
(starts, hides the food and turns round.)

Gleich, Meister! Hier!
Yes, Master! here!

Die
The

stacc. scherzando

Schuh' sind ab-ge-ge-ben in Herrn Beckmesser's Quar-tier.
shoes were taken ear-ly to Mas-ter Beckmesser's house.

Mir war's, als
Methought just

rieft ihr mich e-ben?
now that you called me?

(bei Seite)
(aside)

Er thut,
To-day,

als säh' er mich
he seems not to

(Er nähert sich, sehr demüthig, langsam Sachs.)
(He approaches Sachs very humbly and slowly.)

nicht? Da ist er bös', wenn er nicht spricht!
see! He does not speak: then he is cross!

Immer zurück-

poco rall.

espress.

P.   ✛

27327

DAVID.

Wenn ihr mich schlagt, streichelt sie mich, und lä-chelt da-bei hold so-lig-
When you are harsh, then she is kind; her smiles will drive all care from my

lich; muss ich ca - ri - ren, füt-tert sie mich, und ist in Al-lem gar lie-be-
mind; when I am fast-ing, food she will bring, and she is lovely in ev'-ry

lich! Nur gestern, weil der Jun - ker ver-sungen, hab' ich den Korb ihr nicht ab-ge-rungen. Das
thing! But last night, when she learned the knight's failure, nought would she let me take from her basket. That

schmerzte mich: Und da ich fand, dass Nacht's Einer vor dem Fenster stand, und sang zu ihr,
hurt me sore: and when I found that late, one before her window stood, and sang to her,

Etwas schneller werdend.

Belebter

357

27327

zusammen und geht in die Kammer ab.)
gether and goes into the chamber.)

(Sachs, immer noch den Folianten auf dem Schoose, lehnt sich, mit untergestütztem Arm, sinnend darauf:
(Sachs, still with the folio on his lap, leans with his arms resting upon it; his talk with David does not

es scheint, dass ihn das Gespräch mit David gar nicht aus seinem Nachdenken gestört hat.)
seem to have disturbed his meditation.)

SACHS.

Wahn! Wahn! Ue - ber-all
Craze! Craze! Ev' - ry-where

(Posaune)

sehr weich

Wahn! Wo-hin ich for-schend blick' in Stadt-und Welt-chro-nick, den Grund mir auf-zu-
craze! In vain my looks I cast o'er pre-sent things and past, the rea-son e-ver

Streng im Zeitmass.

fin-den, wa-rum gar bis aufs Blut die Leut' sich quä-len und schin-den in un-nütz tol-ler
seeking, why men so fiercely fight; each one his ma-lice wreaking in aimless frenzied

27327

SACHS.

Wuth? Hat keiner Lohn noch Dank da-von: in Flucht ge-schla - gen wähnt er zu ja - gen;
spite! He wins no wage for all his woe: and flee-ing, dreams he chases his foe: his
ausdrucksvoll.

p   poco cresc.

hört nicht sein ei - gen Schmerzgekreisch, wenn er sich wühlt in's eig'ne Fleisch, wähnt
out-cry of pain he doth not hear, when he him-self his flesh doth tear, ex -

più cresc.   *f*   dim.

Lust sich zu er - zei-gen! Wer gibt den Na-men an? 'sist halt der al - te
ult-ing in his anguish! Ah, who shall tell its name? the craze is still the

(kräftig.)
(loud.)

più p   *pp*   1

Wahn, ohn' den nichts mag ge-schehen, 'smag ge-hen o - der ste-hen! Steht's wo im
same: nought happens here with-out it, howe'er we go a-bout it. Stayed in its

f   *marc.*   *p dolce*   *più p*

27327

SACHS.

Lauf, er schläft nur neu - e Kraft sich an: gleich wacht er auf, dann
course, in sleep re-turns its strength a - gain: and with new force it

schaut, wer ihn be - mei - stern kann!
wakes_ ah, who can hold it then!

Etwas beschleunigend.

Ruhig wie vorher.

Wie friedsam treu - er
With peace-ful ways con-
stacc.

Sit - ten, ge - trost in That und Werk, liegt nicht in Deutschlands
tented, and help-ful work in hand, my Nür-em-burg lies

u.s.w.

SACHS.

Mit - ten mein lie - - bes Nü - ren -
plant - ed a - midst_____ our fa - ther -

(Er blickt mit freudiger Begeisterung ruhig vor sich hin.)
(He gazes before him in joyful enthusiasm.)

berg!
land!

sehr breit

più cresc.

ff

sehr gehalten

Doch ei-nes A - bend's spat, ein Un - glück zu ver-
But on an even-ing late, to safe - guard from dis-

Etwas weniger breit.

dim.

più p

hü - ten bei ju - gend-hei - ssen Ge - mü - then, ein Mann weiss sich nicht
as - ter, and youth-ful pas-sion to mas - ter, a man, fighting with

Immer etwas belebend.

stacc.

p

marc.

poco cresc.

Bass espressivo

27327

SACHS.

Rath; ein Schuster in seinem Laden zieht an des Wahnes Faden: wie bald auf Gas-sen und
fate; a shoemaker at his leather pulls at the craze's tether: then soon his neighbours a-

Immer lebhafter.
stacc.

Strassen fängt der da an zu ra - sen! Mann, Weib, Ge-
wa - ken, by rage and pas - sion sha - ken! Man, wife, and

poco cresc.

sell und Kind, fällt___ sich da an wie toll und blind; und
youth and child, blind - - ly fall to as though gone wild; and

più f

will's der Wahn ge-seg-nen, nun muss es Prü - gel reg-nen, mit Hieben, Stoss' und
mad - ness brings its blessing, of strife and blows un-ceasing, re-peating, aye, the

Noch mehr belebend.

p

marc. *cresc.* *stacc.*

SACHS.

Dreschen den Wu-thesbrand zu löschen.
story, to quell the ra-ging fury.

Gott weiss, wie das ge-
God knows how that be-

schah?
fel!

Sehr mässig.

Ein Ko-bold half wohl da:
A ko-bold wove the spell.

ein
In

Glühwurm fand sein Weibchen nicht;
vain his mate a glow-worm sought;

der
'twas

27327

ge-lin - - - gen.
be - gin - it.

Zweite Scene.
Second Scene.

(Walther tritt unter der Kammerthüre ein. Er bleibt einen Augenblick dort stehn, und blickt auf Sachs
Dieser wendet sich und lässt den Folianten auf den Boden gleiten.)
*(Walther enters by the chamber door. He pauses there a moment and looks at Sachs, who turns and lets
the book slide to the floor.)*

SACHS.

Grüss'Gott, mein Junker!
Sir knight, I greet you!

Ziemlich bewegt.

WALTH.

(sehr ruhig)
(very quietly)

Ein we-nig, a - ber
A lit-tle, but my

Ruh-tet ihr noch! Ihr wach-tet lang,nun schlieft ihr doch?
Lay you till now?Though late to bed, you slept, I trow?

merk'. Glaubt mir, des Men-schen wahr-ster Wahn wird ihm im Trau - me auf - ge-
lurk. Be - lieve! our deep - est wis - dom here is oft in dreams to us made

than: all' Dichtkunst und Po - e - te - rei ___ ist nichts,
clear. All po - ems that the world has known ___ are nought

als Wahr - traum - deu - te - rei. Was gilt's, es gab der Traum euch
but truths ___ our dreams have shown. Perchance your dream may shew the

ein, wie heut' ihr sol - let Mei - ster sein?
way to win the Master's prize to - day!

WALTH.
(sehr ruhig) (very quietly)

Nein, von der Zunft und ih - ren Meistern wollt sich mein Traumbild nicht be-
Nay, from your guild and all its Masters, my dream would bring me new dis-

pp dolce

piu p

P. u. c.

P.

(etwas lebhafter)
(with more animation)

geistern.
as-ters.

Wie
How

SACHS.

Doch lehrt' es wohl den Zauberspruch, mit dem ihr sie ge-wännet?
Yet might it teach the magic spell that makes the master-singer.

espress.

dolce

poco cresc. mf

t. c.

P.

wähnt ihr doch nach sol-chem Bruch, wenn ihr noch Hoffnung kennet!
bold your heart, since what be-fel, if in it hope still linger!

Die Hoffnung lass' ich mir nicht
With hope my heart is e - ver

p

sf

p cresc.

P.

mindern, nichts stiess sie noch über'n Haufen; wär's nicht, glaubt, statt eu're Flucht zu hindern, wär'ich
beating, and thence hope shall not be driven; were't not so, ne'er had I stayed your flitting; but my-

f

dim.

p

cresc.

P.

27337

P.

selbst mit euch fort-ge-laufen! Drumbitt'ich, lasst den Groll jetzt ruh'n! Ihr habts mit
self as your guide had given! So, pray you, let your an-ger go: you have with

Eh - ren männern zu thun; die ir - ren sich und sind bequem, dass man auf ih - re
men of hon-our to do: mistakes they make, and each w'd find in o-ther men the

Wei - se sie nähm': Wer Preise er - kennt, und Prei - se stellt, der will am
thoughts of his mind: and fair'tis that they who grant a prize should ask what

End' auch, dass man ihm ge - fällt. Eu'r Lied, das hat ih - nen bang ge-
seemeth goodly in their eyes. Your song has filled them with dark dis-

SACHS.

Freund, in hol - der Ju - gendzeit, wenn uns von mächt'gen Trie-ben zum
friend, when youth's de - sires compel, and'twards the goal of lov-ing the

sel'gen ersten Lie - ben die Brust sich schwellet hoch und weit, ein
soul is surely mov - ing,whenhearts with passion beat and swell, the

schö - nes Lied ———— zu sin - genmocht'vielen da ge - lin - gen: der Lenz,
boon of song ———— by Hea - ven to many then is giv - en: 'tis spring

der sang für sie. Kam
that sings, not they. Through

27327

SACHS.

Sommer, Herbst und Win-ter-zeit, viel Noth und Sorg' im Leben, manch'
summer, fall and winter's spell, when life hath brought its burden, with

eh-lich Glückdaneben: Kindtauf', Geschäfte, Zwist und Streit: denen's
marriage joy asguerdon: children, misfortune, strife as well: they to

dann noch ___ will ge - lin - gen ein schö - nes Lied zu
whom then ___ still by Hea - ven the grace of song is

sin - gen, seht: ___ Mei - - ster nennt man
giv - en, as ___ Mas - - ters live for

lei - ten, und hel-fen wohl bewah-ren, was in den Ju-gend Jah-ren, mit
lead you, and help to keep untaint-ed what spring and youth have planted a-

hol - dem Trie - be Lenz und Lie - be euch un-be-
midst youth's plea - sures; so the trea - sures,deep in the

p molto cresc. *dim.*

(zart)(*tenderly*)

wusst in's Herz ge-legt, dass ihr das un- - ver-lo - ren
heart in se - cret laid, through might of song shall ne - ver

dolce *p* *più p*

WALTH.

Steh'n sie nun in so ho - hem
Tell me, then, if so high they

hegt! *fade!*

p cresc. *f* *p*

27837

27327

(Walther hat sich zu Sachs am Werktisch gesetzt,wo dieser das Gedicht Walther's nachschreibt.)
(Walther has placed himself by the working bench near Sachs who writes down Walther's poem.)

Mässig langsam.

(sehr lange)

WALTH.

(anschwellend)
(cresc.)

"Mor-genlich leuch-tend in ro - si-gem Schein von Blüth' und Duft geschwellt die
"Bathed in the sun-light at dawn of the day, when blossoms rare made sweet the

(Nicht schleppend)
dolcissimo
poco cresc.

(voll)
(f)

Luft, voll al - ler Won - nen, nie er-son-nen, ein Gar-ten lud mich ein, Gast ihm zu
air, with beauties teem - ing, past all dreaming, a glorious garden lay, cheering my

molto cresc.

sein."
way."

SACHS.

Das war ein "Stollen;" nun ach-tet wohl, dass ganz ein gleicher ihm
That was a "Stanza," and take good heed; an - o - ther like it must

27327

390

392

SACHS.

Reim' und Tö - nen reich; dass man's recht schlank und selb-stig find', das freut die
be both rhyme and tone. Let it be shape - ly found and neat; such child-ren

Ael-tern an dem Kind; und eu - ren Stol-len giebt's den Schluss, dass nichts davon ab-fal-len
parents gladly greet; your stanzas so will find an end, and all things to-gether will

WALTH.

„Sei euch ver -
"How shall I

muss.
blend.

traut, welch'hehres Wunder mir ge-scheh'n: an meiner Sei - te stand ein Weib so hold und
name the radiant wonder there re-vealed? A woman fair my vi - sion blessed; her peer no

(zart)
(softly)

P.   ✦

27327

WALTH.

schön ich nie ge - seh'n: gleich ei - ner Braut um - fass - te sie
mor - tal e'er be - held: *bride-like she came, and fold - ed me*

sanft _____ mei - nen Leib, ___ mit Au - gen win-kend, die Hand wies
fast _____ on her breast; then gent - ly rais-ing her hand, and

blin-kend, was ich ver-lan - gend be-gehrt, die Frucht so hold und werth vom Le -
gaz-ing where gleamed the fruit's golden hue, she shewed the place where grew the tree ___

- bens - - - baum."
of _____ life."

poco rall. Mässig bewegt.

SACHS (gerührt.)
(moved.)

Das nenn' ich mir ei - nen Ab-gesang! Seht wie der gan-ze Bar gelang! Nur mit der Me-lo -
In sooth, I call that an Af-ter song! See how the verse now flows along! But with the me-lo -

dei seid ihr ein we - nig frei: doch sag' ich nicht dass das ein Feh - ler sei;
dy are you a lit - tle free. Yet say I not that that's a fault with me:

nur ist's nicht leicht zu be-hal-ten, und das är-gert uns' - re Al - ten.
but for the ear 'tis perplexing, and to old men that - is vex - ing.

Jetzt richtet mir noch ei - nen zwei-ten Bar, damit man merk' welch' der er - ste war. Auch
A se-cond verse must you now compose, to fix in mind how the first one goes. And

396

WALTH.

däm-mert der Blick mir sich bricht: wie weit so nah' be-schienen da zwei lich-te
round me and darkens the place: a-far yet near, two stars ap-pear, in day's de-

cresc. - - - - -

Ster-ne aus der Fer-ne, durch schlanker Zwei-ge Licht, hehr mein Ge-sicht.
clin-ing,soft-ly shining, where branches in-ter-lace, down on my face.

mf dim. - - - più p pp poco cresc.

P. ✛ P. ✛ P. ✛ P. ✛

Lieb-lich ein Quell auf stil-ler Hö-he dort mir rauscht; jetzt schwellt er
There on a height, a bubbling fountain at my feet, from earth out-

p cresc. -

an sein hold Ge-tön', so stark und süss ich's nie er-lauscht: leuchtend und
pours its lim-pid stream, with swelling tone, so full and sweet. Sparkling and

f dim. -

P. P. ✛

27327

SACHS.

zie - - ret sein, wenn's Statt - li - ches zu
fore us now; by dar - - ing deeds to

wa - - - gen gilt. Drum
reach our ends. So

kommt, seid ihr gleich mir ge - sinnt.
come, if you and I are friends.

(Walther schlägt in Sachsen's Hand ein, so geleitet ihn dieser ruhig festen
Schrittes zur Kammer, deren Thüre er ihm ehrerbietig öffnet, und dann ihm folgt.)
(*Walther grasps Sachs's hand, who leads him with a quiet, firm step to the.*
chamber door, opening it for him respectfully and then following him.)

Weniger breit.

(Man gewahrt Beckmesser, welcher draussen vor dem Laden erscheint, in grosser Aufgeregtheit
(*Beckmesser appears outside the shop window, looking in, in great perturbation. Finding the shop*

Von hier etwas zu beschleunigen.

Immer mehr be-

hereinlugt, und da er die Werkstatt leer findet, hastig hereintritt.)
empty he enters hastily.)

schleunigen.

Dritte Scene.
Third Scene.

BECKM. (Er ist sehr aufgeputzt, aber in sehr leidendem Zustande.)
(*He is dressed very richly, but seems very miserable.*)
(Er blickt sich erst unter der Thüre nochmals genau in der Werkstatt um.)
(*He peeps again carefully round the shop from the doorway.*)

Sehr mässig.

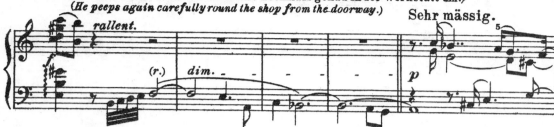

(Dann hinkt er vorwärts, zuckt aber zusammen, und streicht sich den Rücken.)
(*He then limps forwards, winces in pain
and rubs his back.*)

(Er macht wieder einige Schritte, knickt aber
mit den Knien, und streicht nun diese.)
(*After a few more steps forward his knees give
way. He rubs them.*)

(Er setzt sich auf den Schusterschemel, fährt aber
schnell schmerzhaft wieder auf.)
(*He sits on the cobbler's stool, but starts up again
in pain.*)

(Er betrachtet sich den
(*He contemplates the stool,*
Etwas lebhaft und im-

Schemel und geräth dabei in immer aufgeregteres Nachsinnen.)
and his thoughts appear to become increasingly agitated.)
mer mehr belebend.

(Er wird von den verdriesslichsten Erinnerungen und Vorstellungen gepeinigt; immer unruhiger be-
(*He is distressed by the most grievous memories and fancies; getting ever more uneasy, he begins*

27327

ginnt er sich den Schweiss von der Stirne zu wischen.)
to wipe the perspiration from his brow.)

(Er hinkt immer lebhafter umher und starrt dabei vor sich hin.)
(He limps round more and more restlessly, staring before him.)

(Als ob er
(As if pursued

von allen Seiten verfolgt wäre, taumelt er fliehend hin und her.)
from all sides, he stumbles hither and thither as in flight.)

Immer schneller.

(Wie um nicht umzusinken hält er sich an dem Werktisch, zu dem
er hingeschwankt war, an, und starrt vor sich hin.)
*(As though to save himself from falling he holds on to the table, to
which he has tottered, and stares before him.)*

Sehr schnell.

405

27827

406

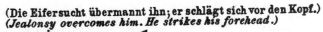
(Die Eifersucht übermannt ihn; er schlägt sich vor den Kopf.)
(Jealonsy overcomes him. He strikes his forehead.)

(Er glaubt die Verhöhnung der Weiber und Buben auf der Gasse zu
(He fancies that he hears again the mocking of the women and boys

vernehmen, wendet sich wüthend ab, und schmeisst das Fenster zu.)
in the alley; turns away in a rage and slams the window to.)

(Sehr verstört wendet er sich mechanisch wieder dem Werktische zu, indem er
(Much disturbed he turns mechanically again to the work-table which he con-

vor sich hinbrütend, nach einer neuen Weise zu suchen scheint.)
templates as he appears to be seeking a new tune.)

407

27327

SACHS.

deu-ten; eu-re Hochzeit spuk-te unter den Leu-ten: je
mind you; and a bride to-day the folk have assigned you: The

cresc. stacc.

p p stacc. cresc.

P. P.

(wüthend.)
(furiously)

BECKM.

Oh,
Oh,

tol - ler es da her-geh', je bes - ser be-kommt's der Eh'!
mad - der the fun, you see, the bet - ter your luck will be! Schnell.

ff

P.

Schu - - ster voll von Rän - ken und pö - - - bel-haf - ten
cob - - bler full of cun - ning, with brain_____ on tricks e'er

f f f f

P. P. P. P.

Schwänken! Du warst mein Feind von je: nun hör', ob hell ich seh'.___ Die
running! You e - ver were my foe, and now your craft I know.___ The

ff sehr kurz p cresc. ff p

P.

BECKM.

ich mir aus er-ko-ren, die ganz für mich ge-bo-ren, zu al-ler WittwerSchmach der
maid for whom I've wait-ed, for me a-lone cre-a-ted; all wid-ow-ers to shame, on

stacc.

p

cresc.

Jungfer stellst du nach. Dass sich Herr Sachs er-wer-be des Goldschmieds reiches Er-be, im
her you fix your aim! 'Tis Mas-ter Sachs's pleasure, to win the goldsmith's treasure, and

f   *p*   stacc.   *p*

Meisterrath zur Hand auf Klau-seln er be-stand; ein Mägdlein zu be-thö-ren, das
so be-fore the Guild, our ears with stuff he filled; a maiden's fan-cy fool-ing, that

p   *p*

nur auf. ihn sollt' hö-ren, und Andern ab-gewandt zu ihm al-lein sich fand.
she might heed his schooling, and, to the shame of all, her choice on him might fall.

p   *p*   *p*   *f*

P.   +   P.   +   P.   +   *f*

27327

Singen, merkt auf wie's mag ge - lin-gen!
semble, to-day your voice may tremble.

Bin ich ge - zwackt auch und zer -
Though I am thwacked, laugh not too

hackt, euch bring'ich doch si-cher aus dem Takt.
soon, for I will yet put you out of tune.

SACHS.

Gut Freund, ihr seid in ar - gem Wahn;_ glaubt was ihr
Good friend, your wits are o - ver - cast.__ Think what you

Sehr allmählich in der Schnelligkeit nachlassend.

wollt, dass ich ge-than; gebt eu're Ei-fer-sucht nur hin; zu wer-
will of what is past: be not through jealou - sy so blind; for woo-

Hier bereits mässige Bewegung.

BECKM.

Lied? / song?

Nun denn? / Well then?

SACHS.

Der fehlte wohl, wer da-rauf rieth'! / Who counts on that, indeed is wrong!

Wie doch? / How now?

_pp_

poco cresc.

Ihr fragt? / You ask?

Dass ihr mit aller / That you with all your

Was noch? / What more?

più cresc.

_f_

_p_

Bie-der-keit der ärg-ste al-ler Spitzbuben seid. / pro-bi-ty the worst of rogues for ev-er will be.

Mag sein; / May be;

più p

_p_

dolce

P. ✛ P. ✛

SACHS.

doch hab' ich noch nie entwandt, was ich auf frem-den Tischen fand: und / but yet I was ne-ver known to take up things I did not own. And

P. ✛ P. ✛ 27827 P. ✛ P. ✛

SACHS.

dass man von euch auch nicht Üb-les denkt, behal-tet das Blatt, es sei euch ge-
men for this act-ion might call you thief! To save you from that, I give you the

BECKM. (in freudigem Schreck aufspringend.)
(spinging up in joyful surprise.)

Herr Gott! Ein Ge-dicht?
Good Lord! A song?

schenkt.
leaf.

glissando

gliss.

Ein Gedicht von Sachs?
A song by you?

Doch halt',
Yet stay,

gliss.

dass kein neuer Schad' mir erwachs'!
lest mis-hap should cross me anew!

Ihr habt's wohl schon recht gut memo-
The song you have, no doubt, got by

poco riten.

BECK.

rirt?
heart?

SACHS.

Ihr lasst mir das Blatt?
You give me the song?

Seid mei-net-halb doch nur un-be-irrt!
Fear not that my claim your plan will thwart.

Da-
Lest

a tempo.

espress.

p

dolce

t.c. P. P.

Und mach' ich Ge-brauch?
To use as I like?

Doch sing' ich das Lied?
The song I may sing?

mit ihr kein Dieb.
thief you should be.

Wie's euch belieb'.
I leave you free.

Wenn'snicht zu
If you know

p

poco cresc.

P. P. P.

4 5

Und, wenn ich gefiel'?
And if I succeed?

(Ganz zutraulich.)
(With complete trust.)

Da
Ah,

p

schwer.
how.

Das wunder-te mich sehr.
'Twould startle me, I trow.

dim.

più p

pp

p

P. P.

(Gleichsam pfeifend.)
(Whistles.)

seid ihr nun wieder zu be-scheiden; ein Lied von Sachs,
now you fail to prize yourself du-ly. A song by Sachs!

das will was be-
That means something,

p

1 1 1

> p

p

27327

BECKM.

deu - ten. Und seht nur, wie mir's er - geht, wie's mit mir Ärmsten
tru - ly. And look you! sad is my plight, since the ills of the

steht! Er-seh' ich doch mit Schmerzen, das Lied, das
night, with heart ach-ing and doubting, when-e'er I

Nachts ich sang, Dank eu'ren lust'gen Scherzen! es machte der Pog - nerin
think on my lay. Thanks to your foolish flouting, the maiden was filled with dis-

bang'. Wie schaff'ich mir nun zur Stel - le ein neu - es
may. How can I, with all my learning, now make a -

SACHS.

und gelob' es euch: nie mich zu rühmen, das Lied sei von
and my oath I give; ne'er will I claim it, so long as I

dim. più p poco riten.

BECKM. (sich vergnügt die Hände reibend.)
(rubbing his hands with delight.)

Was will ich mehr? Ich bin ge - bor-gen: jetzt braucht sich Beckmesser
What would I more? Ill-luck is o - ver: Beck - mes - ser now will hence-

mir.
live.

sf pp cresc.

P.

nicht mehr zu sor - gen.
forth live in clo - ver.

Doch, Freund, ich führ's euch zu Ge - mü - the,
But, friend, now deem me not a scoff - er,

stacc. 5 stacc.

f p f

P. ✦ P. ✦

und rath' es euch in al - ler Gü - te: studirt mir recht das
if coun - sel good to you I of - fer: to con the song with

sempre stacc.

p

27327

SACHS.

Lied; sein Vor - trag ist nicht leicht; ob euch die
heed; not ea - sy 'tis to sing. The "mode" may

poco a poco cresc.

Wei - se ge - rieth', und ihr den Ton er - reicht.
fail at your need, the "tone" may false - ly ring.

p cresc.   f

P.

BECKM.

Freund Sachs, ihr seid ein gu-ter Po-et; doch was Ton und Wei-se be-trifft, gesteht, da
Friend Sachs, as po - et, first is your place, but when "tones" and "modes" are in hand, confess, that

sf   pp   p

thut mir's Kei - ner vor. Drum spitzt nur fein das Ohr, und:
I need have no fear. Then o - pen well your ear, and:

riten.

cresc.   f   p   più p   pp   f

P.   P.

27327

426

BECKM.

"Beckmesser! Keiner besser!"
"Beckmesser! Tone-professor!"

Darauf macht euch ge-fasst,
And all your doubt will cease,

wenn ihr mich ruhig singen
if you let me but sing in

poco riten..

lasst.
peace.

Doch nun memo-ri-ren, schnell nach Haus:
But now I must learn it well by heart:

oh-ne Zeit zu ver-
that no time may be

a tempo (lebhaft.)

lie - ren richt' ich das aus.
wast-ed, I must de-part.

Hans Sachs, mein Theu-rer, ich
Hans Sachs, my comrade, your

hab' euch ver-kannt;
heart I mis-read;

durch den A - ben-teu - rer war ich ver-
by the knight of Stolz-ing I was mis-

27327

427

27827

Fer-se.
fire.
A - de! Ich muss fort: an andrem Ort dank' ich euch
Fare-well! I must go: we meet a-gain. Thanks in sin-

in - niglich, weil ihr so min - niglich; für euch nur stim- me ich, kauf' eu - re
cer - i - ty take for your friend-li-ness; you shall my vote command, all of your

Wer - ke gleich, ma-che zum Mer - ker euch, doch fein mit Krei-de weich, nicht mit dem
works I'll buy, you shall our Mark - er be, but on-ly chalk we use; mark not with

Ham-merstreich! Mer-ker! Merker! Merker Hans Sachs!
hammer blows! Marker! Marker! Marker, Hans Sachs!

BECKM.

Dass Nürn - berg schus - ter-lich blüh' und
That Nürn - berg e - ver may bloom and

p stacc.   cresc.

wachs'!
wax!

Vl.

u.s.f.

f stacc.

P.

(Beckmesser nimmt tanzend von
(Beckmesser, dancing about, takes

Sachs Abschied, taumelt und poltert der Ladenthüre zu; plötzlich glaubt er das Gedicht in seiner
leave of Sachs and hurries stumbling to the door; suddenly the thinks he has forgotten to pocket

più f   stacc.   ff

Tasche vergessen zu haben; läuft wieder vor, sucht ängstlich auf dem Werktische, bis er es in der
the song, comes forward again and anxiously seeks it on the table, until he discovers it in his

Vl.
Br.
ff
ff

Cb. in 8va.

eigenen Hand gewahr wird: darüber scherzhaft erfreut, umarmt er Sachs nochmals, voll feurigen Dankes,
hand; delighted thereat, he again embraces Sachs, in fervent gratitude, and then rushes, limping and stum-

und stürzt dann, hinkend und strauchelnd, geräuschvoll durch die Ladenthüre ab.)
bling noisily, through the shop door.)

Vierte Scene.

(Eva reich geschmückt, in glänzend weisser Kleidung, etwas leidend und blass, tritt zum Laden herein, und

Fourth scene.

(Eva richly dressed in gleaming white, rather sad and pale, enters the shop and comes slowly forward.)

SACHS.

blieb'!
be?

Grüss'Gott, mein Ev'chen! Ei, wie herrlich und
Good day, my Ev'chen! Ei, art arming thy-

Mässig.

p dolce / *poco cresc.* / *tr*

schreitet langsam vor.)

stolz du's heute meinst!
self with weavons fine,

Du machst wohl Alt und Jung begehrlich,
both old and young by beauty charming,

mf ausdrucksvoll. / *dim.*

wenn du so schön er-scheinst.
that thou so bright dost shine?

EVA.

Meister, 's ist nicht so ge-fährlich: und
Mas-ter, 'tis not so a-larming: though

p dolce

27327

434

EVA.

ist's dem Schneider geglückt, wer sieht dann, wo's mir beschwerlich, wo still der Schuh mich
all be well with a dress, some fault yet the foot may be harming, un-seen the shoe may

poco rallent.

cresc.

drückt?
press.

SACHS.

Der bö-se Schuh! 's war deine Laun', dass du ihn gestern nicht probirt.
The wicked shoe! The fault was thine, that yester-day thou triedst them not.

riten.   *a tempo.*

ausdrucksvoll.   *fp*   *più p*

EVA.

Merk' wohl, ich hatt' zu viel Ver-trau'n; im Meister hatt' ich mich ge-
Mark you, too firm a faith was mine! The mas-ter was not all I

p

irrt.
thought.

Sobald ich
Whene'er I

SACHS.

Ei, 's thut mir leid! Zeig' her, mein Kind, dass ich dir hel-fe gleich geschwind.
If grieves me sore; come here to me; that I may help thee, let me see.

cresc.   *dim.*   *p*

27327

436

EVA.
sagt' ich ja:
there, I know:

drum drückt er mich an den Ze - hen da.
'tis on my toes that it hurts me so.

SACHS.

Hier links?
Here left?

Nein rechts.
No, right.

Hier mehr am Hacken.
More on the instep.

Ach,
Ah,

Wohl mehr am Spann?
Here at the heel?

Kommt der auch dran?
What there as well?

Meister!
Mas-ter!

Wüsstet ihr besser als ich, wo der Schuh mich drückt?
Know you, then, bet-ter than I where the shoe doth pinch?

sehr ausdrucksvoll.

sfp   cresc. —

Ei!
I

(Walther in glänzender Rittertracht, tritt unter die Thüre der Kammer.)
(*Walther in shining knightly costume enters by the chamber door.*)

's wun - dert mich, dass er zu weit,
won - der why, if 'tis too broad,

und doch drückt über - all!
it still pinches you so!

molto cresc. —

P.   P.   P.

27327

437

(Sachs hat Eva sanft den Schuh vom Fusse gezogen; während sie in ihrer Stellung verbleibt, macht er sich am Werktisch mit dem Schuh zu schaffen, und thut als beachte er nichts Anderes.)

SACHS *(Sachs had gently drawn Eva's shoe from her foot; she remains in the same position, as he takes the shoe to the work-table and works at it as if taking note of nothing else.)*

Ruh'.
past.

p dolce

p

(bei der Arbeit.
(working.

Immer schustern, das ist nun mein Loos; des Nacht's des Tags, kom' nicht davon los.
Cobbling always, that now is my lot; by night, by day, my toil ceases not.

Kind, hör' zu: ich hab' mir's ü-ber-dacht, was meinem Schustern ein En-de
Child, give heed, and hear what I have thought: my cobbling must to an end be

mf dim.

p

macht: am besten ich wer-be doch noch um dich; da ge-wänn' ich doch was als Po-et für
brought; and haply 'twere best to ven-ture for thee, then some profit as po-et were won for

cresc. *mf dim.* *p*

27327

SACHS.

mich.   Du hörst nicht drauf? So sprich doch jetzt; hast mir's ja selbst in den Kopf ge-
me,   Thou hear'st me not? Now speak a word; for first the plan from thy lips I

setzt!   Schon gut!   _ich merk'_   „mach' dei-ne
heard.   'Tis well!   I see!   "Make but thy

Schuh'!"   Säng' mir nur wenigstens Ei-ner da-zu!   Hör-te heut' gar ein schönes
shoes!"   If I could only now summon my muse!   Lately a beauteous song I

Lied: wem da-zu wohl ein drit-ter Vers ge-rieth?
heard: would but some one now sing me verse the third!

27327

WALTH. (den begeisterten Blick unverwandt auf Eva geheftet.)
(gazing in rapture on Eva.)

Weil-ten die Ster - ne im lieb - li-chen Tanz? So licht und
Lured from their dan - ces the stars glided down, and sparkled

klar im Lo-cken-haar, vor al-len Frau - en hehr zu schauen, lag ihr mit zar - tem
fair a-bout her hair; on her at - tend-ing, beauty lending, and round her head there

Glanz ein Ster - nen-kranz!
shone a star - ry crown.

Wun - der ob
Won - der on

SACHS (immer fort arbeitend)
(still working)

Lausch', Kind! Das ist ein Mei-ster-lied.
Hark, child! that is a Mas-ter-song.

Wun - der nun bie - ten sich dar: zwie-fa - chen Tag ich grüssen
won - der was born on the height: ere night was gone a two-fold

27327

442

WALTH. (Sachs hat den Schuh zurück gebracht, und ist jetzt darüber her ihn Eva wieder an den Fuss zu ziehen.
(Sachs has brought back the shoe and is now occupied in fitting it again on Eva's foot.)

min - nig und mild sie flocht ihn um das Haupt dem Ge-
Ten - der her mien, as her hand wove its leaves round my

mahl: dort Huld - ge - bo - ren, nun Ruhm er-
head: where love hath bound me, there fame hath

SACHS.
Nun schau, ob da-zu mein Schuh ge-rieth? Mein' endlich doch,
Now see if as well my shoe will pass. At last, I trow,

ko - - ren, giesst pa-ra - die - si-sche Lust sie in des Dichter's
crowned me: I drink from her radiant eyes all joys of pa-ra-

es thät' mir ge-lin-gen? Versuch's, tritt auf!
my la-bour has prospered? Now try, stand up!

Brust im Lie - - - - - - - - - bes-
dise, in love's fair

Sag', drückt er dich noch?
Say, how is it now?

27827

WALTH.

443

traum!
dream.

(Eva, die wie bezaubert regungslos gestanden, gesehen und gehört hat, bricht jetzt in
(Eva, who has stood motionless as if enchanted, gazing and listening, now passion-

Sehr lebhaft.

heftiges Weinen aus, sinkt Sachs an die Brust, und drückt ihn schluchzend an sich. Walther ist zu ihnen getre-
ately bursts into tears, sinks on Sachs's breast, and presses herself to him, sobbing. Walther has come to them;

ten; er drückt begeistert Sachs die Hand. Sachs thut sich endlich Gewalt an, reisst sich wie unmuthig los, und
he presses Sachs's hand. Sachs at length controls himself and tears himself moodily away; and so leaves Eva

SACHS.

lässt dadurch Eva unwillkürlich an Walther's Schulter sich anlehnen.)
involuntarily leaning on Walther's shoulder.)

Hat
A

27327

SACHS.

An-dern zu eng';
that one too small.
von al-len Sei-ten
To all his neighbou
Lauf' und Gends-man and

dräng': da klappt's, da schlappt's, hier drückt's, da zwickt's; der
thrall. Too loose, too tight, too thick, too slight. The

Schuster soll auch Al-les wissen, flicken was nur im-mer zer-ris-sen:
cobbler must have wit un - ending, patching all the holes that need mending:

und ist er gar Po - et da-zu, da lässt man am End' ihm auch da kei-ne Ruh';
and if he be a po - et too, no rest can he find then, but toil e-ver new;

SACHS.

Pech,— und gilt für dumm; tückisch und frech.
place!— they call him dull, knavish and base.

Ei! 'sist mir nur um den Lehr-bu-ben leid; der ver-liert mir al-len Respekt: die
Ah! I am grieved for the prentice, I say: all re-spect he loses for me: for

Le — ne macht ihn schon nicht recht gescheit, dass aus Töpf' und Tellern er leckt. Wo Teu-fel er
Le — ne spoils him by night and by day, and a la-zy glutton is he. The de-vil now

EVA (indem sie Sachs zurückhält und von Neuem an sich zieht.)
(as she holds Sachs back and again draws him to her.)

O Sachs!— Mein Freund! Du
O Sachs!— My friend! My

jetzt nur wie-der steckt!
knows where he can be!

EVA.

nicht? Durch dich ge - wann ich, was man preis't; durch dich er -
me. *Through thee my wis - dom I have won; through thee my*

sann ich, was ein Geist; durch dich er - wacht', durch dich nur
spi - rit I have known; through thee I live, through thee I

dacht' ich, e - del, frei und kühn;_____ du_____
strive: and, no - ble, brave and free thy_____

lies - sest mich er - blüh'n!_____
spi - rit grew in me_____

Ein wenig breiter.

450
EVA.

Ja, lie-ber Meister, schilt mich nur;
Aye, dearest Master, chide at will;

ich war doch auf der rech-ten
my fan-cy was the right one

Spur. Denn, hatte ich die Wahl, nur dich erwählt'ich mir; du wa-rest mein Ge-
still; and if I had a voice, and were my heart my own; 'tis thou would'st be my

mahl, den Preis ———— reicht' ich ———— nur
choice, the prize ———— were thine ———— a -

dir. Doch nun hat's mich ge -
lone. But now I feel a

Erstes Zeitmass.

27327

451

27327

452

27327

SACHS.

koren. So ist's nach Meisterweis' und Art, wenn ei-ne Mei-ster-wei - se ge-schaf-fen
mated. This is by use the Masters' right— when e'er a Mas-ter-mode has been brought to

ward, dass die ei-nen gu-ten Na-men trag', d'ran Je - der sie er-ken-nen
light, the strain by a goodly name they call, and so hence-forth 'tis known to

mag. Vernehmt, re-spek-ta-ble Ge - sell - - schaft,
all. Now know, worthy people, who hear me,

was euch hier zur Stell' schafft! Ei-ne Meisterwei-se ist ge-
why I call you near me. Here a "Mastermode" was fashioned

SACHS.

lun-gen, von Junker Wal - ther ge-dich-tet und ge-sun-gen: der jungen Wei-se le-ben-der
newly: and by this knight has been sung be-fore us du-ly: he asks that we our aid now may

Va-ter lud mich und die Pog-ne-rin zu Ge - vat - - - - -
lend him, and straight at its bap-tism here at - tend _____

- ter.
him.

weil wir die Wei-se wohl ver-nommen
As to his song our ears have listened,

sind wir zur Tau-fe hier-her ge-kom-men; auch dass wir zur Handlung Zeu-gen ha-ben, ruf'
we hith-er come that it may be christened. That we who have heard at - test its fitness, let

ich Jungfer Lene und mei - nen Kna - - - - ben.
David and Lene now stand to___ wit - - - ness.

Doch da's zum Zeu-gen kein Lehr-bu - be thut, und heut auch den Spruch er ge-sun-gen
But as no prentice a wit-ness may be, and right well to-day he has sung to

gut, so mach' ich den Burschen gleich zum Ge-sell'. Knie' nie-der, David, und nimm die-se
me, a jour-ney man I will make of him now. Kneel, David, and, on thy knees, take this

(David ist niedergekniet;
Sachs giebt ihm eine starke Ohrfeige.)
*(David has knelt;
Sachs gives him a smart box on the ear.)*

Schell'. Steh' auf, Ge - sell', und
blow. *A - rise, the blow thou*

mon legato

458 SACHS.

Deut - wei- se" sei sie ge - nannt zu des Mei - sters Prei- se.
dream - sto - ry;" *so be it called, to its Mas - ter's glo - ry.*

Nun wach-se sie gross, ohn'Schad'und Bruch. Die jüngste Ge - vat-te - rin spricht den
And let it both far and wide be heard. I leave to the god-mother now the

(Er tritt aus der Mitte des Halbkreises, der von den Uebrigen um ihn gebildet worden war, auf
die Seite, so dass nun Eva in der Mitte zu stehen kommt.)
*(He moves from the middle of the half-circle which the others have formed round him, so that
Eva stands now in the middle.)*

Spruch.
word.

EVA.

Se - - lig,wie die Son - ne mei-nes Glü - ckes lacht,
Bright - ly as the sun up-on my for - tune breaks,

Langsam, doch leicht fliessend.

p dolciss.

460

27327

P.

(Eva und Magdalene gehen)
(Eva and Magdalene go)

(zu Walther)
(to Walther)

SACHS.

Gleiche Bewegung (♩=♪)

p stacc.

Nun, Jun-ker, kommt! Habt fro-hen
Now come, Sir knight! Your ills are

Muth! David, Ge-sell': schliess' den La-den gut!
past. David, lock up: leave all safe and fast!

(Als Sachs und Walther
(As Sachs and Walther

p

sempre stacc.

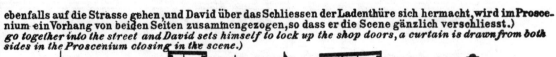

ebenfalls auf die Strasse gehen, und David über das Schliessen der Ladenthüre sich hermacht, wird im Proscenium ein Vorhang von beiden Seiten zusammengezogen, so dass er die Scene gänzlich verschliesst.)
go together into the street and David sets himself to lock up the shop doors, a curtain is drawn from both
sides in the Proscenium closing in the scene.)

un poco cresc.

Allmählich etwas belebter im

Zeitmass.

27327

(Hörner auf dem Theater, entfernt aufgestellt und sehr stark geblasen.)
(*Horns on the stage, distant and very loudly played.*)

(Trompeten auf dem Theater, den Hörnern
(*Trumpets on the stage, opposite the Horns.*)

entgegengesetzt.)

27327

468

Fünfte Scene.

Die Vorhänge sind nach der Höhe aufgezogen worden; die Bühne ist verwandelt. Diese stellt einen freien Wiesenplan dar, im fernen Hintergrunde die Stadt Nürnberg. Die Pegnitz schlängelt sich durch den Plan; der schmale Fluss ist an den nächsten Punkten praktikabel gehalten. Bunt beflaggte Kähne setzen unablässig die ankommenden, festlich gekleideten Bürger der Zünfte, mit Frauen und Kindern, an das Ufer der Festwiese über. Eine erhöhte Bühne, mit Bänken und Sitzen darauf, ist rechts zur Seite aufgeschlagen; bereits ist sie mit den Fahnen der angekommenen Zünfte ausgeschmückt; im Verlaufe stecken die Fahnenträger der noch ankommenden Zünfte ihre Fahnen ebenfalls um die Sängerbühne auf, so dass diese schliesslich nach 3 Seiten hin ganz davon eingefasst ist. Zelte mit Getränken und Erfrischungen aller Art begrenzen im Uebrigen die Seiten des vorderen Hauptraumes.

Vor den Zelten geht es bereits lustig her: Bürger, mit Frauen, Kindern und Gesellen, sitzen und lagern daselbst. — Die Lehrbuben der Meistersinger, festlich gekleidet, mit Blumen und Bändern reich und anmuthig geschmückt, üben mit schlanken Stäben, die ebenfalls mit Blumen und Bändern geziert sind, in lustiger Weise das Amt von Herolden und Marschällen aus. Sie empfangen die am Ufer Aussteigenden, ordnen die Züge der Zünfte, und geleiten diese nach der Sängerbühne, von wo aus, nachdem der Bannerträger die Fahne aufgepflanzt, die Zunftbürger und Gesellen nach Belieben sich unter den Zelten zerstreuen. So eben, nach der Verwandlung, werden in der angegebenen Weise die Schuster am Ufer empfangen, und nach dem Vordergrund geleitet.

Fifth Scene.

The curtains have been drawn up and a new scene represents an open meadow with the town of Nuremberg in the distance. The Pegnitz, a narrow stream, practicable at its nearest part, winds across the stage. From gaily decorated boats which arrive continually at the bank, Burghers of the guilds, with women and children in festival costume, land on the meadow. A raised platform with chairs and benches on it has been erected on the right, decked with the banners of those Guilds which have already arrived. As new Guilds come on, their banner-bearers also plant their banners around the platform so as finally to close it in entirely on 3 sides. Tents with drinks and refreshments of all kinds on sides of stage.

In front of the tents there is merry making; Burghers with women and children and Journeymen sit and lie about there. Prentices of the Mastersingers, richly decked with flowers and ribbons, with slender staves similarly adorned, merrily act the parts of heralds and marshals; they receive the new arrivals on the shore, order the processions of Guilds and lead them to the singers' platform, whence, after the banner-bearers have planted the banners, the Burghers and Journeymen disperse as they please at the booths. As the curtains rise the Shoemakers are being thus received at the bank and conducted to the front.

469

470

gu - te Zeit, macht' ih - nen war - me Schuh'; und
mer - ry time; well shod from toe to heel; if

gu - te Zeit, macht' ih - nen war - me Schuh'; und
mer - ry time; well shod from toe to heel; if

gu - te Zeit, macht' ih - nen war - me Schuh'; und
mer - ry time; well shod from toe to heel; if

gu - te Zeit, macht' ih - nen war - me Schuh'; und
mer - ry time; well shod from toe to heel; if

wenn ihm Kei - ner 's Le - der leiht, so stahl er sich's da -
lea - ther lacked, he thought no crime, and stole what he could

wenn ihm' Kei - ner 's Le - der leiht, so stahl er sich's da -
lea - ther lacked, he thought no crime, and stole what he could

wenn ihm Kei - ner 's Le - der leiht, so stahl er sich's da -
lea - ther lacked, he thought no crime, and stole what he could

wenn ihm Kei - ner 's Le - der leiht, so stahl er sich's da -
lea - ther lacked, he thought no crime, and stole what he could

27327

472

27327

(Gesellen mit Kinderinstrumenten.)
(Journeymen with toy instruments.)

Trompeten a.d.Theater. (Trumpets on the stage.)
Stadtwächter und Heerhornbläser. (Town watchmen and Trumpeters.)

Rührtrommeln (a.d.Theater.)

474

27327

DIE SCHNEIDER.
THE TAILORS.

477

DIE SCHNEIDER.
THE TAILORS.

27327

478

DIE SCHNEIDER.
THE TAILORS.

Me-e-e-e-e-e-eck! Me-e-e-e-e-e-eck! Me-e-e-e-e- - - - - - -
ble-e-e-e-e-e-eat! ble-e-e-e-e-e-eat! ble e e e e - - - - - -

Me-e-e-e-e-e-eck! Me-e-e-e-e-e-eck! Me-e-e-e-e- -
ble-e-e-e-e-e-eat! ble-e-e-e-e-e-eat! ble-e-e-e-e- -

Me-e-e-e-e-e-eck! Me-e-e-e-e-e-eck! Me-e-e-e-e- -
ble-e-e-e-e-e-eat! ble-e-e-e-e-e-eat! ble-e-e-e-e- -

Me-e-e-e-e-e-eck! Me-e-e-e-e-e-eck! Me-e-e-e-e- -
ble-e-e-e-e-e-eat! ble-e-e-e-e-e-eat! ble-e-e-e-e- -

eck! Wer glaubt's, dass ein Schnei-der, ein Schneider, ein Schneider im Bo-cke
eat! Who'd think that a tai - lor, a tai - lor, a tai - lor would have such

eck! Wer glaubt's, dass ein Schnei-der, ein Schneider, ein Schneider im Bo-cke
eat! Who'd think that a tai - lor, a tai - lor, a tai - lor would have such

eck! Wer glaubt's, dass ein Schnei-der, ein Schneider, ein Schneider im Bo-cke
eat! Who'd think that a tai - lor, a tai - lor, a tai - lor would have such

eck! Wer glaubt's, dass ein Schnei-der, ein Schneider, ein Schneider im Bo-cke
eat! Who'd think that a tai - lor, a tai - lor, a tai - lor would have such

479

27327

480

DIE BÄCKER.
THE BAKERS.

gäb'euch der Bä-cker nicht täg-lich Brod, müsst' al — — le Welt ver -
bakers must bring us our dai-ly bread, or hun — — ger soon would

gäb'euch der Bä-cker nicht täg-lich Brod, müsst' al — — le Welt ver -
bakers must bring us our dai-ly bread, or hun — — ger soon would

gäb'euch der Bä-cker nicht täg - lich Brod, müsst' al — — le Welt ver -
bakers must bring us our dai-ly bread, or hun — — ger soon would

gäb' nicht der Bä - cker Brod, müsst' al — — le Welt ver -
bak - ers must bring us bread, or hun — — ger soon would

schei — — den. Beck! Beck! Beck! Täg-lich auf dem
end us. Wheat, wheat, wheat, makes the bread we

schei — — den. Beck! Beck! Beck! Täg-lich auf dem
end us. Wheat, wheat, wheat, makes the bread we

schei — — den. Beck! Beck! Beck! Täg-lich auf dem
end us. Wheat, wheat, wheat, makes the bread we

schei — — den. Beck! Beck! Beck! Täg-lich auf dem
end us. Wheat, wheat, wheat, makes the bread we

27327

(Ein bunter Kahn mit jungen Mädchen in reicher bäuerischer Tracht kommt an. Die Lehrbuben laufen nach dem Gestade.)
(A decorated boat arrives full of young girls in rich peasants dresses. The Prentices run to the bank.)

27327 P.

484

(Das Charakteristische des folgenden Tanzes, mit welchem die Lehrbuben und Mädchen zunächst nach dem Vordergrund kommen, besteht darin, dass die Lehrbuben die Mädchen scheinbar nur am Platz bringen wollen; sowie die Gesellen zugreifen wollen, ziehen die Buben die Mädchen aber immer zurück, als ob sie sie anders wo unterbringen wollten, wobei sie meistens den ganzen Kreis, wie wählend, ausmessen, und somit die scheinbare Absicht auszuführen anmuthig und lustig verzögern.)

(The peculiarity of the following dance with which the Prentices and girls come to the front, is this: the Prentices apparently only wish to bring the girls to the open place, but, as the Journeymen keep trying to seize the girls, the Prentices draw them away as if seeking to take them to another place, whereby they make the tour of the whole stage, continually delaying their original purpose in good-natured fun.)

Mässiges Walzer-Zeitmass.

(David kommt vom Landungsplatze vor und sieht
(David comes forward from the landing place and

missbilligend dem Tanze zu.)
looks disapprovingly at the dancing.)

27327

DAVID.

Ihr tanzt? Was werden die Meister sagen? (Die Lehrbuben
You dance? *Be- ware lest the Masters hear it?* drehen ihm Nasen.)
(The Prentices make
fun of him.)

Hört nicht? Lass' ich mir's auch be - ha - gen. (David nimmt sich ein
You laugh? *Well then, I too will dare it.* (David seizes a pretty

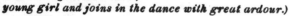

junges schönes Mädchen, und geräth im Tanze mit ihr
schnell in grosses Feuer.)
young girl and joins in the dance with great ardour.)

ALT.

LEHRBUBEN. PRENTICES.

Die
Thy

1.TENOR. (Die Lehrbuben winken David.)
(The Prentices make signs to David.)

David! Die
David! *Thy*

2.TENOR.

Da-vid! (Die Zuschauer freuen sich
Da-vid! und lachen.)
(The onlookers laugh.)

486

LEHRBUBEN. / PRENTICES.

Le-ne sieht zu.
Le-ne looks on.

(David, erschrocken, lässt das Mädchen schnell fahren, um welches
die Lehrbuben sogleich tanzend einen Kreis schliessen; da er Lene
nirgends gewahrt, merkt David, dass er nur geneckt worden, durch-
bricht den Kreis, erfasst sein Mädchen wieder, und tanzt nun noch
feuriger weiter.)
(David, startled, quickly lets the girl go. The prentices directly dance
in a circle round her. As David does not see Lene any-where, he realizes
that he has been fooled, and, breaking through the circle, he seizes the
girl again and dances on more ardently.)

Le-ne sieht zu.
Le-ne looks on.

Le-ne sieht zu.
Le-ne looks on.

Die Le - ne sieht zu.
Thy Le - ne looks on.

sempre ff

DAVID.

Ach! lasst mich mit euren Possen in Ruh'!
Ah! Cease fool-ing now, and leave me a - lone!

(Die Buben suchen ihm das Mädchen zu entreissen, er wendet sich mit ihr jedesmal glücklich ab, so dass nun ein
(The Prentices try to pull the girl away from him; he always manages to evade them, so that a similar

cresc.

ähnliches Spiel entsteht wie zuvor, als die Gesellen nach den Mädchen fassten.)
performance takes rise to that above described, where the Journeymen try to seize the girls.)

cresc.

cantabile

27327

27327

488

(Die Meistersinger ordnen sich am Landungsplatze zum festlichen
Aufzuge.)
(At the landing-place the Master-singers arrange themselves for
a grand procession.)

(Beginn des Aufzuges
der Meistersinger.)
(*The Master-singers'
procession starts.*)

(Hier kommt Kothner mit der Fahne im Vordergrunde an. Die geschwungene Fahne, auf welcher König Da-
(Here Kothner reaches the front with the banner bearing the portrait of king David with his harp, at sight of

vid mit der Harfe abgebildet ist, wird von allem Volk mit Hutschwenken begrüsst.)
which the people wave their hats.)

(Der Zug der Meistersinger ist hier auf der Singerbühne, wo Kothner die Fahne aufgepflanzt, angelangt:
Pogner, Eva an der Hand führend, diese von festlich geschmückten und reichgekleideten Mädchen, unter
denen auch Magdalene, begleitet, voran.)
(*The procession of the Master-singers has now reached the platform, where Kothner plants the banner: Pogner
leading forward Eva by the hand. She is accompanied by girls richly dressed; among them is Magdalene.*)

(Trompeten auf dem Theater.)
(*Trumpets on the stage.*)

(Als Eva, von den Mädchen umgeben, den mit Blumen geschmückten Ehrenplatz eingenommen, und alle
Übrigen, die Meister auf den Bänken, die Gesellen hinter ihnen stehend, ebenfalls Platz genommen,
treten die Lehrbuben, dem Volke zugewendet, feierlich vor der Bühne in Reih' und Glied.)
*(When Eva, surrounded by the girls, has taken the flower strewn place of honour and all the rest are
in their places, the Masters on the benches, the Journeymen standing behind them, the Prentices ad-
vance to the platform in proper order and turn round to the people.)*

495

+) Ausser Sachs singen alle Anwesenden diese Strophe mit: sie
ist daher, je nach der Stimme in jede Gesangsparthie einzutragen.
(Alle Sitzenden erheben sich; die Männer bleiben mit entblös-
tem Haupte. Beckmesser bleibt, mit dem Memorirendes Ge-
dichtes beschäftigt, hinter den andern Meistern versteckt, so
dass er bei dieser Gelegenheit der Beachtung des Publikums
entzogen wird.)

+) All present except Sachs join in this strophe, taking parts
according to their voices.
(All those sitting rise; the men standing with bared heads.
Beckmesser, hidden behind the other Masters, is busy trying to learn the song by heart, unobserved by the public.)

27327 P.

497

27827

498

+) Von hier an singt der Chor des Volkes wieder allein; die Meister auf der Bühne, so wie die andern vorigen Theilnehmer am Gesange der Strophe, geben sich dem Schauspiele des Volksjubels hin.

+) *From here the chorus of people sing alone: the Masters and other characters take part in the rejoicings of the people.*

(Das Volk nimmt wieder eine jubelnd bewegte Haltung an.)
(The people resume their jubilation.)

P. 27327

SACHS (der unbeweglich, wie geistesabwesend, über die Volksmenge hinweg geblickt hatte, richtet endlich seine Blicke vertrauter auf sie, und beginnt mit ergriffener, schnell aber sich festigender Stimme.)
(*who motionless, as if wrapt in thought, has been gazing far away over the crowd, at length turns his eyes with kindly expression on them and begins in a voice at first veiled by emotion but quickly becoming firmer.*)

Euch macht ihr's leicht, mir macht ihr's schwer, gebt ihr mir Armen zu viel Ehr'!
Words light to you bow me to earth: your praise is far beyond my worth.

27827

27327

502

SACHS.

ehrt, da galt es zu be - wei-sen, dass,wer ihr selbst gar an-ge-
you, I fain would show you clearly, that one who lives her servant

hört, sie schätzt ob al - len Prei - sen. Ein Meister,reich und hoch-ge-
true o'er all doth love her dear - ly. A Master rich and high in

muth, der will heut' euch das zei - gen: sein Töch - - ter
worth, his love now lets you mea - sure: his daugh - - ter

lein,___ sein höch - - stes Gut, mit al - lem Hab' und
fair,___ his best___ on earth, with all his gold and

P. 27327

503

27327

SACHS.

traut,___ euch ruf' ich's vor dem Vol - - ke laut:
day,___ to you be - fore all folk I say:

erwägt der Wer - bung selt'nen Preis, und wem___ sie soll ge -
think well how rare___ a prize is here, that each___ may surely

lin - gen, dass der sich rein und e - del weiss im
bring her a heart and voice both pure and clear, as

SACHS.

Wer———ben wie im Sin———gen, will er das Reis er-
suit———or and as sing———er. *Let this yourhearts em-*

rin-gen, das nie,———— bei Neu-en noch bei Al——ten, ward je so
bold-en; that ne'er———— in pres-ent times or old——en, wascrownso

herr——lich hoch ge-hal-ten, als von der lieb——lich
no——bly high up-hold-en, as by this maid——en

27327

SACHS.

Rei — nen, die nie — mals soll be — wei — — nen,
ten — — der; may fate from harm de — fend her,

cresc. — — — — — —

P.   P.   P.

dass Nü — ren — berg mit höch — stem Werth die for
that Nü — rem — berg her voice may raise

P.   P.   P.

Kunst und ih — re Mei — — — — — ster
Art, and in her Mas — — — — — ters'

P.   P.   P.

27327

508

BECKM.(zu dem sich jetzt Sachs wendet, hat schon während des Einzuges, und dann fortwährend, eifrig das Blatt mit dem Gedicht herausgezogen, memorirt, genau zu lesen versucht, und oft
verzweiflungsvoll sich den Schweiss getrocknet.)
*(to whom Sachs now turns, has all through been constantly taking the poem from his
pocket and trying to learn it by heart, often wiping the sweat from his brow in
despair.)*

27327

510

BECKM.

Das Lied, bin's sicher, zwar Niemand versteht; doch bau' ich auf eu-re Po-pu-la-ri-
The song by no-one will be understood; but I build upon your favour with the

SACHS.

geht!
see!

dim.   *cresc.*

tät.
crowd.

Nun denn, wenn's Mei-stern und Volk be - liebt,____ zum
Then now, if Masters and peo - ple will,____ at

fp stacc. *cresc.* *f*

KOTHN.

(hervortretend.)
(*advancing.*)

Ihr le - dig' Mei - ster!
Un - mar - ried Mas - ters,

SACHS.

Wett - ge-sang man den An-fang giebt.
once the sing - ers may prove their skill.

Hb.

p Hr.

p *cresc.* *p*

P. ✠

514

515

27327

516

27327

(Beckmesser,der sich endlich mit Mühe auf dem Rasenhügel festgestellt hat,macht eine erste Verbeugung gegen
die Meister,eine zweite gegen das Volk, dann gegen Eva, auf welche er,da sie sich abwendet,nochmals verle _
(Beckmesser,who with trouble has at length found firm footing on the mound,bows first to the Masters,
then to the people and then to Eva, at whom, when she turns away, he again blinks with embarrassment; he

gen hinblinzelt; grosse Beklommenheit erfasst ihn; er sucht sich durch ein Vorspiel auf der Laute zu ermuthigen.)
tries to calm his uneasiness by a prelude on the lute.)

BECKM.

LAUTE.

„Mor-gen ich leuchte in
"Bathing in sunlight at

(„Mor - gen - lich leuch-tend in
("Bathed in the sun-light at

ro - si-gem Schein, von Blut und Duft geht schnell die Luft; wohl bald ge-won - - nen, wie zer-
dawning of day,   with bo-som bare,   to greet the air;   my beauty steam - ing,   fast er

ro - si-gem Schein,   von Blüth und Duft   ge-schwellt die Luft,   voll al-ler Won - - nen,   nie er-
dawn of the day,   when blos-soms rare   made sweet the air,   with beauties teem - - ing,   past all

ron - - nen;   im Gar-ten lud _____ ich ein   garstig und fein."
dream - - ing;   a gar-den round - - - e-lay   wearied my way."

son - - nen,   ein Gar-ten lud _____ mich ein,   Gast ihm zu sein.")
dream - - ing,   a gar-den round _____ me lay,   cheer-ing my way.")

27327

518

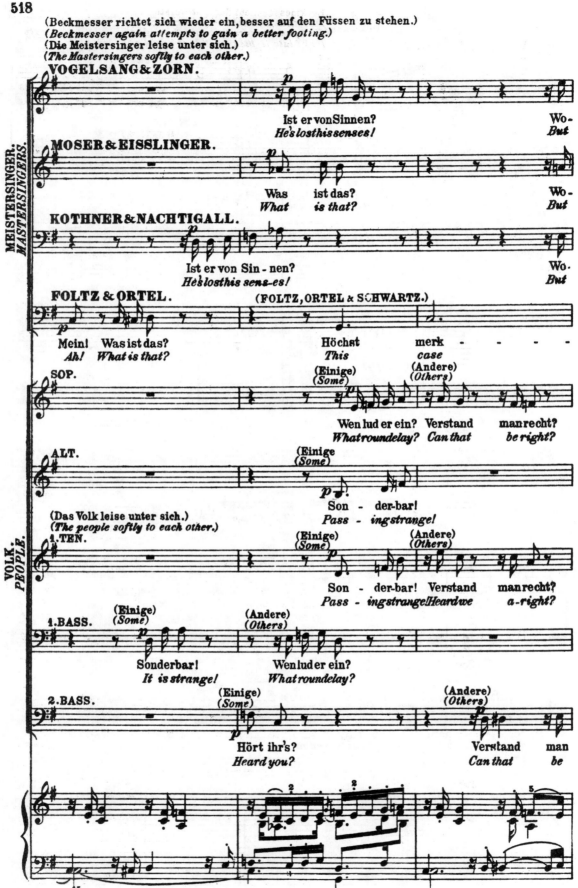

519

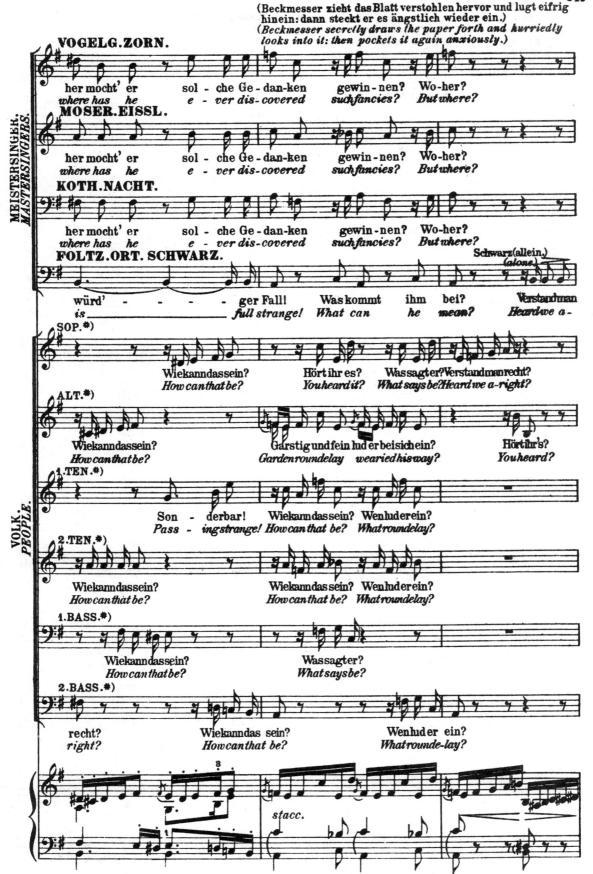

*) Die verschiedenen Stimmen abwechselnd.

27327

521

27327

BECKM. (rafft sich verzweiflungsvoll und ingrimmig auf.)
(he rouses himself with an effort of despair and rage.)

„Heimlich mir graut,— weil es hier
"What is her name? *What radiant*

LAUTE.

(„Sei euch ver-traut,— welch' heh-res
("How shall I name— the radiant

Mässig.

poco rall. accel. tr tr

fp cresc. f

dim.

(r.)

p f

munter will hergeh'n: an mei-ner Lei-ter stand ein Weib; sie
thunder clearly pealed? *A woman's hair in fash-ion dressed:* *with*

Wun-der mir ge-scheh'n: an mei-ner Sei-te stand ein Weib, so
won-der there revealed? A wo-man fair my vis-ion blessed; her

p cresc. f dim.

schämt und wollt' mich nicht be - - seh'n;— bleich wie ein Kraut um-
clear im-mort-al air it swelled. *Brid-ling she came, and*

schön und hold ich nie ge - - seh'n; gleich ei - ner Braut um-
peer no mort al e'er be - held: bride-like she came, and

p cresc. - - f dim. p tr

P.

27327

BECKM.

LAUTE.

fa-sert mir Hanf mei-nen Leib;
fold-ed me there in a chest;

fass - te sie sanft mei - nen Leib
fold - ed me there to her breast

mit Au-gen zwinkend
in-tent-ly gaz-ing,

mit Au - gen then, gent - ly

zwinkend win-kend, rais-ing

der Hund blies
her hound was

die Hand wies her hand and

accelerando

winkend,
grazing

blin - kend gaz - ing

was ich vor lan - gem verzehrt,
and gleaned the roots old and new:

was ich ver - lan - gend be-gehrt, where gleamed the fruit's gold - en hue,

wie
she

die she

Frucht so Holz und
sowed the space with

Frucht so hold und showed the place where

accelerando

cresc.

(Alles bricht in ein dröhnendes Gelächter aus.)
(All break ont into mocking laughter.)

Pferd vom Le - ber - - baum!"
rue, the seed of strife!"

werth vom Le - bens - - baum!") grew the tree of life.")

Schnell

(Beckmesser verlässt wüthend den Hügel und stürzt auf Sachs zu.)
Beckmesser in fury leaves the mound and rushes towards Sachs.)

f stacc.

BECKM.

Verdammter Schu - ster, das dank' ich dir! Das
Ac-cursed cob - bler, yours the de - sign! The

Lied, es ist gar nicht von mir: vom Sachs der
song, in sooth, is none of mine: 'twas Sachs whom

hier so hoch ver - ehrt, von eu - rem Sachs ward mir's be - scheert. Mich hat der
ye so much re - vere, that wrote the song I sang you here! Now through his

Schänd - li - che be - drängt, sein schlechtes Lied mir auf - ge - hängt.
shame - ful trick I see! His worth - less stuff he puts on me.

(Er stürzt wüthend
(He rushes away

27327

SACHS.

Von hier an merk-

Beck - mes - ser irrt, wie dort so hier.
Beck - mes - ser errs, both here and there.

Sehr ruhig.

lich langsamer geworden.

Wie er da - zu kam, mag selbster sagen; doch möcht'
Let him now to all tell where he got it; for my-

ich nie mich zu rüh - - men wa - gen, ein Lied,
self, I dare not boast _____ I wrote it; nor yet

so
that

schön wie dies er - dacht, sei von mir Hans Sachs ge-
aught so no - bly fine as this song could e'er be

27327

530

SACHS.

Ich sag' euch Herrn, das Lied ist
I tell you, Sirs, that song is

SOP.

Er sagt das nur zur Lust.
He says it but in jest.

ALT.

macht Spass! Er sagt es nur zur Lust.
makes fun! He says it but in jest.

TEN.

macht Spass! Er sagt es nur zur Lust.
makes fun! He says it but in jest.

1. BASS.

macht Spass! Er sagt es nur zur Lust.
makes fun! He says it but in jest.

2. BASS.

Spass! Er sagt's nur zur Lust.
fun! He says that in jest.

VOLK.
PEOPLE.

mf

P.

SACHS.

schön; nur ist's auf den er-sten Blick zu er-seh'n, dass Freund Beckmesser es ent-
fine; but at first it is not hard to di-vine that friend Beckmesser sang it

p dolce

p

P.

stellt! Doch schwör' ich dass es euch ge - fällt, wenn rich-tig Wort und
wrong. Yet swear I, ye will like the song if now, by one a-

mf

p

27327

SACHS.

Wei - se hier Ei - nersäng' im Krei - se; und wer dies ver -
mong you, the words be right-ly sung you; and he who that

stünd' zu-gleich be - wies', dass er des Lie - des Dich - ter und
truth can bring to light, will prove him - self the po - et and

gar mit Rech - te Mei - sterhiess', fänd' er ge-rech - te Rich - ter.
Mas - ter-sing - er, too, by right: all who have ears will know it.

Ich bin ver - klagt, und muss be - steh'n: drum lasst mich mei-nen
I am ac - cused, and take my stand: my wit - ness let me

poco rallent.

27327

SACHS.

Zeu-gen aus-er-seh'n. Ist Je-mand hier, der Recht mir weiss? Der tret' als
call, then, here at hand." If one to prove my words be here, let him as

Zeug' in die-sen Kreis!
wit-ness now ap - pear!

(Walther tritt aus dem Volke hervor und begrüsst
(*Walther steps forward from the crowd, greets Sachs,*

Sachs, sodann nach den beiden Seiten hin die Meister und das Volk mit ritterlicher Freundlichkeit. Es ent-steht sogleich eine angenehme Bewegung. Alles weilt einen Augenblick schweigend in seiner Betrachtung.)
and then the Masters and the people in turn, with knightly courtesy. A movement of pleasure takes place. All remain silent for a short time, observing him.)

SACHS.

So zeu - get,
Bear wit - ness,

534

SACHS.

das Lied sei nicht von mir; und
this song is none of mine; and

zeu-get auch, dass, was ich hier vom Lied hab' ge-sagt, zu viel nicht sei ge-
wit-ness, too, the song is fine; that all may de-clare, my praise went not too

MEISTERSINGER.
MASTERSINGERS.

VOGELG.

Ei Sachs, ihr seid gar fein! Doch
Ah Sachs, your wit is keen! But

ZORN.

Ei Sachs, ihr seid gar fein! Doch
Ah Sachs, your wit is keen! But

EISSL.

Ei Sachs, wie fein! Doch mag es heut' gesche-hen
Ah Sachs, How keen! But you today again will

NACHT. & KOTH.

Wie fein! Doch mag ___ es heut' ge-
How keen! But you ___ to-day a-

ORTEL & FOLTZ. *p*

Wie fein ___ ist
How keen ___ is

SACHS.

wagt.
far.

cresc. — — *p*

27527

536

538

(An dieser Stelle lässt Kothner das Blatt, in welchem er mit den andern Meistern eifrig nachzulesen begonnen, vor Ergriffenheit unwillkürlich fallen, er und die Uebrigen hören nur noch theilnamvoll zu.)
(Kothner, who with the other Masters had begun to follow the written words of the song, deeply moved, here lets the paper fall. He and the rest listen with interest.)

WALTH.

(wie entrückt.)
(in ecstasy.)

Won - - nen nie er-son-nen, ein Garten lud mich ein, dort un - ter ei - nem
teem - - ing past all dreaming, a garden round me lay, and there be neath a

Wun - der-baum, von Früch - ten reich be - han - gen, zu schau'n in sel' - gem
wondrous tree, where fruits were rich - ly throng - ing, my bliss - ful dream re -

Lie - bestraum, was höchstem Lust - ver - lan - gen Er - fül - lung kühn ver -
vealed to me the goal of all my long - ing, and life's most glor - ious

hiess, das schön - ste Weib: _____ E - va im Pa - ra -
prize, a wo - man fair: _____ E - va in Pa - ra-

(zart.)
(tenderly.)

A - bend-lich düm-mernd um-schloss mich die Nacht; auf stei-lem Pfad war ich ge-
Dark-ness had fall - en___ and night closed me round; on ston-y road my foot-steps

naht zu ei - ner Quel - le rei - ner Wel - le, die
trod, where on a mount - ain rose a fount - ain that

lo - ckend mir ___ ge - lacht: dort un - ter ei - nem
lured my feet ___ with its sound: there un - der - neath a

Lor - beer - baum, von Ster - nen hell durch -
lau - rel tree, where stars like hell fruit were

27327

WALTH.

Tag, dem ich aus Dichter's Traum er - wacht! Das ich er - träumt, das Pa - ra -
day, on which my po-et's dream took flight! That Pa - ra - dise my vision

dies, in himmlisch neu verklärter Pracht, hell vor mir
shewed, revealed a - new in Heaven's light, shin - ing now

lag, da - hin lachend nun der Quell den Pfad mir wies; die
lay; there - to point - ing the path, a laughing streamlet flowed, and

dort ge - bo - ren, mein Herz er - ko - ren, der
gleam - ing yon - der, a ra - diant won - der, the

27327

550

552

POGNER.

27327

554

(Das Volk bricht schnell und heftig in jubelnde Bewegung aus.)
(The people break forth in demonstrations of joy.)

556

(Die Meistersinger feierlich sich zu Pogner wendend.)
(The Mastersingers solemnly turning to Pogner.)
Etwas breiter.
TENOR I & II.
MEISTERSINGER.
MASTERSINGERS.
Auf, Meister Pog - - ner! Euch zum Ruhm, meldet dem
Up, Master Pog - - ner! 'Tis your right, now as a
SOPR.
ALT.
TEN.
BASS.
VOLK.
PEOPLE.
macht.
gained.
Etwas breiter.
f
(mit einer goldnen Kette, daran drei grosse Denkmünzen, zu Walther.)
(with a golden chain, on which are three large medals, to Walther.)
POGNER.
Ge -
King
Junker sein Meis - ter - thum!
Master to name the knight!
P.

558

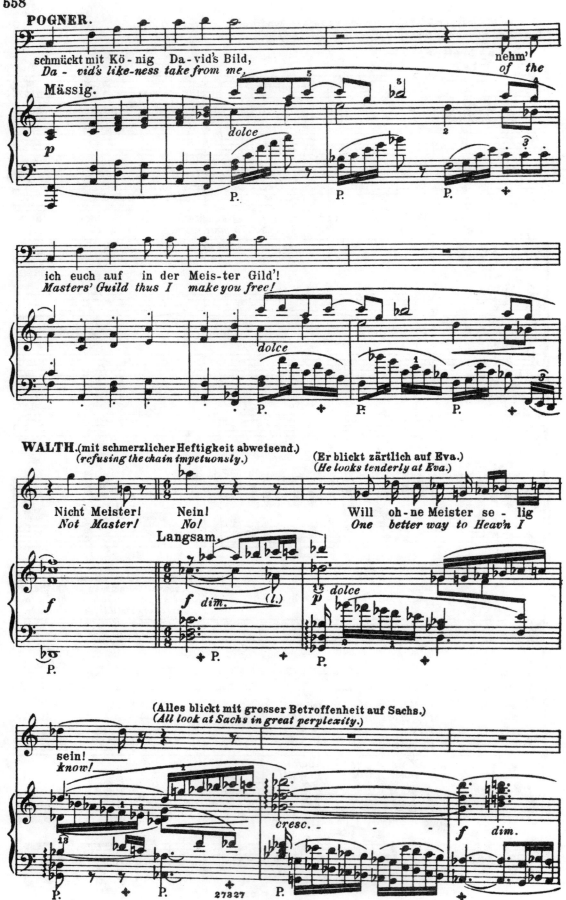

Meis - ter euch ge - freit;
Mas - ter's crown hath won;

dem—— dankt ihr heut' eu'r höch - stes
that—— brings to-day your high - est

cresc.

Glück.
bliss.

Drum denkt mit Dank—— ihr dran zu - rück,
Then think with thank - -ful-ness on this.

wie kann die Kunst wohl
How can that art be

f dim.   p ausdrucksvoll.

P.   +   P   +   gehalten.   P.   +

un - werth sein,
held as naught,

die sol - - che Prei - se schliesset
that prize so rare as this has

cresc.   mf   p   cresc. - -

P.   +   P.   +   P.   +

ein?
brought?

Das uns're Meister sie ge - pflegt grad' recht nach ih - rer
Right well our Masters' Guild did tend our art, and ne - ver

f   p

27327

SACHS.

Art,   nach ih-rem Sin-ne treu ge-hegt, das hat sie echt   be - wahrt: blieb sie nicht
swerved from truth and right to gain their end; thus was our art   pre-served: and though not

stacc.   *poco cresc.*   *poco f*   *p*

ad'- lig, wie zur Zeit, wo Höf' und Fürsten sie ge - weiht;   im Drang der schlimmen
hon-oured as of old, when courts and kings her glories told;   when strife and tur- moil

p   *poco cresc.*

Jahr' blieb sie doch deutsch   und wahr: und wär' sie an-ders nicht ge-
grew, German she stood   and true: and though she veiled her worth-i -

f   *p*

glückt, als wie wo Al - les drängt und drückt, ihr seht wie hoch sie blieb in Ehr':   was
ness, a-mid the mighty storm and stress, you see, her fame is high and sure: what

cresc.   *tr*

P.   +   P.   +   P.   + P.   +

27327

SACHS.

wollt ihr von den Meistern mehr?
would you from the Mas-ters more?

Habt Acht!
Be - ware!

Uns
Ill

dräu - en üb - le Streich':
times now threaten all;

zerfällt erst deutsches Volk und Reich, in
if we Germans should e - ver fall   in

falscher wälscher Majestät kein Fürst bald mehr sein Volk versteht, und wälschen Dunst mit wälschem
thrall to a - ny foreign land, no prince his folk will un-der-stand, and foreign mists will blind our

Tand sie pflanzen uns in deutsches Land; was deutsch und echt, wüsst' Kei-ner mehr, lebt's nicht in
eyes, and o'er our German land will rise: the art we own were lost for aye, liv-ing in

27827

SACHS.

deut - scher Meis - ter Ehr'.　　　Drum　sag' ich euch:
Ger - man song to - day.　　　*Then　hear me now:*

Etwas zurückhaltend.　　　*In das frühere Zeitmass zurückkehrend.*

ehrt　eu - re deut - - schen Meis - ter!　　　Dann
hon - - our your Ger - - man Mas - ters,　　　*if*

bannt ihr gu - - te Geis - ter;　　　und gebt＿＿ ihr　ihrem
you would shun　dis - as - ters;　　　*let each＿＿ hold　them*

27327

Wir - - ken Gunst,   zer-ging' in Dunst   das
deep   in his heart;   then may de - part   the

heil' - ge röm - sche Reich, _____ uns   blie - be gleich   die
pomp of ho - ly   Rome, _____ no   change will come   to

Während des folgenden Schlussgesanges nimmt Eva den Kranz von Wal-
thers Stirne und drückt ihn Sachs auf; dieser nimmt die Kette aus Pogner's Hand, und hängt sie Walther um.
Nachdem Sachs das Paar umarmt, bleiben Walther und Eva zu beiden Seiten
an Sachsen's Schultern gestützt; Pogner lässt sich, wie huldigend auf ein Knie
vor Sachs nieder. Die Meistersinger deuten mit erhobenen Händen auf Sachs,
als auf ihr Haupt. Alle Anwesenden schliessen sich dem Gesange des Volkes an.
*During the following finale Eva takes the wreath from Walther's head
and places it on Sachs, who takes the chain from Pogner's hand, and hangs
it round Walther's neck.*
*After Sachs has embraced the pair, Walther and Eva remain one on each side
of him leaning on his shoulders. Pogner kneels as if in homage before
Sachs. The Mastersingers point to Sachs with upraised hands as to their
chief. All present join in the song of the people.*

heil'ge deutsche Kunst!
ho - ly Ger - man Art!

TENOR.

Ehrt   eu - re deut - schen
Hon - - our   your Ger - man

BASS.

Ehrt   eu - re deut - schen
Hon - - our   your Ger - man

+) Von Allen mitzusingen, schliesslich auch von Walther und Eva.
To be sung by all, finally also by Walther and Eva.

565

VOLK.
PEOPLE.

SOPR. Dann bannt ihr gu-te Geis- / If ye would shun dis-as-

ALT. Dann bannt ihr gu-te Geis- / If ye would shun dis-as-

TEN. Meis- ter, dann bannt ihr gu-te Geis- / Mas- ters, if ye would shun dis-as-

BASS. Meis- ter, dann bannt ihr gu-te Geis- / Mas- ters, if ye would shun dis-as-

-ter; und gebt ihr ih- -rem Wir-ken / -ters; let each one hold them in his

Vl.1. Br. in 8ve / Vl.2. Vc. in 8ve sempre ff / stacc. / etc.

27327

(Als es hier zu der bezeichneten Schlussgruppe
gelangt ist, schwenkt das Volk begeistert Hüte
und Tücher; die Lehrbuben tanzen und schlagen
jauchzend in die Hände.)
(The final tableau is here reached. The people
wave hats and kerchiefs in excitement, the
Prentices dance and joyously clap their
hands.)

SOPR.

heil' - ge deut - sche Kunst, die heil'ge deut - sche Kunst!
ho - ly Ger - man Art, to ho - ly Ger - man Art!

ALT.

heil' - ge deut - - - - - sche Kunst!
ho - ly Ger - - - - - man Art!

1.TEN.

ja ___ die heil' - - - ge deut - sche Kunst!
to ___ our ho - - - ly Ger - man Art!

2.TEN.

heil' - ge deut - - - - - sche Kunst!
ho - ly Ger - - - - - man Art!

BASS.

heil' - ge deut - - - - - sche Kunst!
ho - ly Ger - - - - - man Art!

VOLK.
PEOPLE.

più f

ff

P.   ✛   P.   P.   P.   ✛   ff

SOPR.

Heil!   Sachs!   Nürn - berg's
Hail!   Sachs!   Nürn - berg's

ALT.

Heil!   Sachs!   Nürn - berg's
Hail!   Sachs!   Nürn - berg's

TEN. I & II.

Heil!   Sachs!   Nürn - berg's
Hail!   Sachs!   Nürn - berg's

BASS I & II.

Heil!   Sachs!   Nürn - berg's
Hail!   Sachs!   Nürn - berg's

Vl.2.

Trompeten auf dem Theater.
Trumpets on the stage. ff

ff

P.   ✛ P.   ✛ P.

569

27327